MICHAEL'S
MUSINGS

Also by Michael D. Kurtz

Everyday Life in the Times of the Judges – Included in Abingdon's Bible Teacher Kit

Approaching the New Millennium: Biblical End-Time Images

Lessons from a Christmas Tree Farm: A Devotional and Study Guide Resource

Crossings: Memoirs of a Mountain Medical Doctor

MICHAEL'S
MUSINGS

A Pastor Blogs on Life

Michael D. Kurtz, D Min

iUniverse

MICHAEL'S MUSINGS
A PASTOR BLOGS ON LIFE

iUniverse books may be ordered through booksellers or by contacting:

iUniverse
1663 Liberty Drive
Bloomington, IN 47403
www.iuniverse.com
1-800-Authors (1-800-288-4677)

ISBN: 978-1-4917-4796-4 (sc)
ISBN: 978-1-4917-4797-1 (e)

Printed in the United States of America.

iUniverse rev. date: 09/30/2014

CONTENTS

Dedicated to the church family known as Oak Ridge United Methodist Church, a vibrant and loving community of faith who has taught me and many others much about following and serving Jesus Christ in this world!

1

To know God and To make God known

MAY 14, 2009

There is a line from the Presbyterian Catechism (teachings) that has always caught and held my attention: Our purpose in life is "to know God and to make God known." That is such an awesome motto for a believer's life and living! For me, it summarizes very succinctly our mission and purpose in this world. We are placed on this earth, in this world, to know and experience God and his love, grace and justice. And, not only are we to know God, we are also to make God known to others....so that they too may know and experience his love, grace and justice.

This faith and purpose statement informs and instructs that the Christian life is not about "me and Jesus we got our own thing going" (to quote a bluegrass gospel song). Rather, the Christian life is to be lived in the context of community. And, in addition, this Christian community (church, fellowship, etc.) is to be engaged in outreach and mission in the world. Jesus shares an awesome prayer in John, chapter 17. In it he prays for us in the world. His intimate and instructive prayer includes these words: "Father......I am not asking you to take them out of the world, but to keep them safe from the evil one......" Our culture is often characterized by terms such as individualism and isolationism. Ironically, we have all kinds of high-tech communication devices and yet we can feel so disconnected and alone. It is very difficult to make God known with a posture of isolationism. The incarnation of God in Jesus Christ is in stark contrast to a lifestyle and an attitude of isolation. As followers of Christ, we are insulated (in Jesus Christ) but never isolated from the people and the needs of this world.

While, as Jesus' followers, we are not of the world, we are definitely in the world - placed here to know God and his presence and power in this world and placed here to make God known. How are you doing in your journey to know God? How are you doing in making God known to others?

Scripture: John 3:16-17; John chapter 17.

Reflection: As Christ followers we are to be IN the world but not OF the world.

Prayer: Lord, it is so tempting and easy for us to isolate and separate from the world with all of its problems, complexities and difficulties. Yet, as your people we are called to love all people and to be positive change-agents in the culture in which you have placed and called us to serve. You did not just instruct us to love and serve the world (the people on this earth), but you led by example. Incarnation is the very proof of how much you love the world! God, you entered right into the messiness and chaos of this world! You walked right down the stairway to heaven and placed your baby Son in a manger. And that Son, Jesus the Christ, who became human flesh and blood, walked our earth and experienced all the human emotions, knowing great joy and tremendous loss and grief. You graciously and lovingly did all that so that becoming one with us, we may become one with God. Thank you, Lord. Now may we out of a response of joy and love, go and share and show that same kind of mercy and compassion. In the name of Jesus, God incarnate. Amen

2

Memorial Day Memories

MAY 21, 2009

The author of the Book of Hebrews writes: "Since we are surrounded by such a huge crowd of witnesses to the life of faith, let us strip off every weight that slows us down, especially the sin that so easily hinders our progress......"

This scripture is set in the context of the "roll call" of faith which Hebrews chapter 11 so beautifully presents. Some versions read, "Since we have a grandstand of witnesses cheering us on....." Think of that, persons whom we have known and love. Persons who have positively influenced our life and Christian walk –persons, whom we greatly miss as they have gone on to their heavenly home. These persons, these witnesses, are cheering us on in our Christian journey!

On this Memorial Day Weekend perhaps our thoughts are turned toward those whose presence we miss so much - - family members, loved ones, friends, those who have served on behalf of freedom and liberty, those who taught us about living the Christian faith. Who are you missing? Who are you remembering?

I have a list, as most of us do. I miss my grandparents. I miss my deceased uncles - Paul, Leon and Chester. I miss the two pastors of my childhood days who nurtured me in the faith. I miss my father-in-law, John. And, I still miss my childhood elderly neighbor friend, Hagey Houck. When I was just a young fellow Hagey lived next door to our family and would always have time for this neighborhood kid who frequently showed up at his front door.

Is there someone whom you are greatly missing? Who is "cheering you on?!"

Scripture: Hebrews – chapter 11. Read also Hebrews 12:1-3.

Reflection: Who are the people you miss? And, what about them do you miss most?

Prayer: Thank you, Lord, for the persons you have placed in our lives. Some of them are gone now and we miss them greatly! Yet, there is something of them that lives on in us. Thank you for the memories, some painful and others which bring a warmth to our hearts and smiles to our faces. Yet, all these memories are part of the necessary work and gift of grief. Thank you for the encouragement these departed pilgrims offer our lives. In the name of the Father, the Son, and the Holy Spirit, we pray. Amen

3

The Holy Trinity

JUNE 4, 2009

This Sunday, June 7th, is Trinity Sunday on the Christian calendar. Holy Trinity; Triune God; Three-in-One...Sounds pretty mysterious and difficult, doesn't it? One way to get a handle on this mystery, I believe, comes from a children's Sunday school class. One elementary way to conceptualize the Holy Trinity is to think of water. H2O. Anyway you see it, no matter the form, water still consists of H2O. It may be in the form of a solid (ice); or, gas (vapor); or, liquid (the water we drink). Water is three different forms, yet the same components. It displays various expressions, but same in content.

Of course, something so temporal, such as water, can never adequately explain and define something so mysterious and eternal as Trinity. Yet, this illustration does provide our finite minds with a perspective that can help. God is Father (Yahweh God); God is Son (Jesus the Christ); and, God is Holy Spirit. The Holy Trinity has various manifestations, yet is one and the same. God is frequently referred to as Creator. Jesus Christ is often referred to as Redeemer. And, the Holy Spirit is sometimes called Sustainer. Each is unique in their role(s); yet all three are involved with one another in carrying out these unique and special roles. The ministry of the Holy Trinity is multifaceted. And, the unity of the Trinity is constant and continual. It is like water (water so basic and so essential to life). You get many different manifestations, but it is always one and the same.

The reality of Triune God also reminds me that God is relational. From the very beginning, before time, God has always been in relationship - - - with God's self! There was and there is Father, Son, and Holy Spirit. They are the same, yet separate. Therefore, they relate to one another. They cooperate. They complement. They work together to accomplish and get things done. They delight in one another's presence and being. So too

5

should we as God's people! One of the great messages of Trinity Sunday is that God is relational. God desires to be in relationship with us - humanity. And, we are created in the image of God. Therefore, we crave and need relationship with God and with one another.

May you and yours have a blessed Trinity Sunday, and may we all be reminded of God's multifaceted outreach and God's desire for relational love with each, and all, of us.

Scripture: Matthew 28:19; 2 Corinthians 13:14; I Peter 1:2.

Reflection: The Triune God is Creator, Redeemer, and Sustainer in our lives. What do each of these persons and roles of the Holy Trinity mean to you?

Prayer: Triune God, in the beginning of time you proclaimed, "Let us make humankind in our image." From the very start Creator, Redeemer, and Sustainer, you have been working together to redeem and reconcile humankind and all the earth! From the mercy, love, and complementation of Holy Trinity relationship, O God, may we receive our enlightenment and our empowerment to help bring your kingdom on earth as it is in heaven. May it be so, in the name of the Father, the Son, and the Holy Spirit. Amen

4

Notes from Annual Conference

JUNE 15, 2009

One of the conferences we United Methodists observe each and every year is called Annual Conference. In the Western North Carolina Conference we are probably a bit spoiled since our Annual Conference is held at beautiful and scenic Lake Junaluska Assembly, near Waynesville, NC.

For twenty-seven years now this has been an annual trek for me, to travel to Lake Junaluska and participate in the Annual Conference. Annual Conference consists of: legislative and business sessions; presentation of programs and ministries in and through the WNC Conference; and, services of worship and praise. It is inspiring and impressive, for example, to see and hear over 3,000 delegates gathered together to sing the songs of the faith in Stuart Auditorium! It is icing on the cake to look out the windows of Stuart Auditorium and soak in God's incredibly beautiful creation at Lake Junaluska in the Blue Ridge Mountains!

A United Methodist bishop presides at each of the Annual Conferences. This year we welcomed our new episcopal leader - Rev. Larry Goodpaster. Bishop Goodpaster challenged us as Western North Carolina United Methodists to raise the bar for Jesus as we seek to live out our Conference vision, "Follow Jesus, Make Disciples, Transform the world."

Using three (3) as a reminder symbol, he is casting the vision for:

- 300,000 members in WNC United Methodist Churches, up from the present 293,000.
- 30,000 increase in average worship attendance.
- 3,000 Volunteer in Mission teams going into the world from WNCC congregations.
- 300 re-missioned churches.

- 30 new faith communities.
- All in 3 years (by Dec. 31, 2012).

I pray that our Conference will rise and rally to meet this challenge. And, I pray that Oak Ridge UMC will take part in helping to meet these ministry and mission goals in Jesus' name!

It will require a new perspective for many of us in local churches to enable this vision to be fulfilled. And, yet, it is a first-century perspective, of which Jesus calls us to, which is "Go into all the world and make disciples...." Too many churches for too long have maintained the posture and attitude which says, or implies: "Come and worship and fellowship with us if you want to. But, if you come, remember, we write the rules and you do things our way." These are the kind of churches that repeat the "Seven last words of the dying church" - - "We have never done it that way!" And, of course, the result is a dying congregation.

Instead, the Good News of Jesus Christ calls us, implores us, to reach out to people where they are. The gospel instructs us to rub shoulders with those in our community and world. To show them the love of Jesus Christ by how we treat them and relate to them. And, to try new methods while never changing the Gospel message. We are challenged to experiment with new styles, while never compromising the basic substance of the Good News.

This includes looking at old things in new ways. Our Bishop shared with us in a sermon at Conference an illustration that looks at an old picture in a new way. I found it inspiring and instructional. I hope you do as well. He mentioned that many of our churches have that picture of Jesus Christ holding a lantern and knocking on a door. If you have looked carefully you will see there is no exterior doorknob. For years this has been interpreted as Jesus knocking on the door of our hearts and life and he will not come in until we willingly open the door to allow him entry (Of course this still applies and preaches!). But, perhaps we would consider that in the life of our local churches, Jesus is knocking on the door of our church. And, he is saying "Come out!" "Come out of your church into the world for there is a world that is dying to hear and experience the love and grace of Jesus Christ."

Scripture: Mathew 28:18-20; Acts 1:8.

Reflection: Where is your Jerusalem? Where is your Judea? Where is your Samaria? In what ways are you involved in making a positive difference in this world in Jesus' name?

Forgive us for navel-gazing, Lord. At times all we think about is ourselves – ourselves, our family, our church, our country, our agenda. There is a much bigger world out there than our self-centered world. Help us to think and pray globally while we act locally. May we for your sake bloom where we are planted, while recognizing that how we serve locally affects the entire planet. Open our eyes that we may see the bigger picture. Help us to see what you, O Lord, would have us to see. And, then, help us to serve how and where you want us to serve. In the gracious name of the One in which there is no East or West we pray. Amen

5

Inspiring Worship

JUNE 25TH, 2009

A vision statement serves as a roadmap. It guides us so that we may reach our appointed destination. Oak Ridge UMC's Vision Statement includes five (5) specific components. Five specific areas in which we believe God has called us and gifted and resourced us in the making followers of Jesus Christ. The very first of these five vision components is: INSPIRING WORSHIP.

Worship is the lifeblood of Christians. It is that for which we were created - - to give praise and honor to God. Worship is the one thing we do on earth that we will do forever. As someone wisely states, "Our worship is dress rehearsal for eternity." This raises the bar for me as I consider our worship. Therefore, I affirm we should give our very best to God as we prepare and plan for our corporate worship services.

I give thanks for those who have and are helping us at ORUMC to better plan and prepare and pray for INSPIRING WORSHIP. One of the current ways we are doing this is by hiring an Associate Director of Music Ministries. Under the advisement of our Staff-Parish Relations Committee (hiring arm of the church) and the direction of our Church Council we soon hope to have this music staff person in place. Thanks to our Music Search Committee we were able to survey our congregation as concerns music ministry needs at ORUMC. The surveys were compiled and interpreted and from this congregational feedback our Music Search Committee put together a Music Ministry Path for both the short-term and long-term.

We are incredibly blessed by and thankful for our present music ministry through staff and volunteers. However, through the congregational survey it was overwhelmingly observed that the wish is to grow and enlarge our music ministry at worship. This would enable more persons to share their

God-given music talents and gifts through increased venues during worship services. For example, we plan to add hand bells, and more children and youth music and drama involvement. There is also a desire to share more musical talent and personnel among our various worship services. All this will help strengthen and increase INSPIRING WORSHIP of our Lord and Savior Jesus the Christ.

Scripture: I Chronicles 16:29; Psalm 96:9; John 4:24; Revelation 5:11-12.

Reflection: Worship is the one thing that we do on earth that we will do forever in eternity.

Prayer: Awesome God, our hearts and souls crave worship of you! Forgive us for when we fall prey to idol worship. May we, instead, get lost in wonder, love and praise of you and you alone. When we truly worship you we remember who we are and whose we are. O God, thank you for the gift of worship! Amen

6

Revelation about Victory in Jesus

JULY 1, 2009

Beginning Sunday, July 5th, and for three continuous Sundays, we will be considering the Book of Revelation in our worship services. How difficult and confusing apocalyptical literature can be! Yet, if we do our history lessons, and try as best we can to understand the times in which this literature was written, we can come a long way in gaining insight and renewed inspiration from this incredible Book.

Of course three Sunday sermons will not give us nearly enough time to unpack this book, and only allows us to scratch the surface. Yet, even a scratching of the surface of this great work yields an awesome hope and wonderful assurance for the person who trusts in Jesus Christ. Yes there is battle and blood and pain depicted in the apocalyptic imagery. But, in the final analysis, Revelation assures us that God in Christ defeats Satan and evil and we may now experience that victory through his amazing grace!

Revelation was not written in order to hold threats of damnation before sinners, but to encourage Christians to press on, despite all opposition, despite all evil, and despite all the odds that would say give up and give in. God through Christ has won the war! There are some battles and skirmishes remaining for us, but we are already victorious in and through our Lord! This then enables us and encourages us to live with hope in our daily faith walk!

Scripture: Revelation 15.

Reflection: While there are still some battles and skirmishes, through Christ the battle has been won!

Prayer: All-Powerful God, there seems to be so much in the world that seeks to undo us and upend us. Yet, the truth is that we are in your almighty hands and providential care. May we then, secure in the confidence and assurance of your victory, go out working for justice and mercy in your kingdom. In the victorious name of Jesus we pray. Amen

7

The Best is Yet to Come!

JULY 17, 2009

No matter how many times I've heard it, I love the story told about the lady who asked her pastor to come and see her to discuss her funeral plans. This well prepared lady gave the pastor a list of funeral plans. On the list were included scripture readings, congregational hymns and other special portions for the service. She even had listed the clothing she had selected for her burial. The attentive minister listened and confirmed her plans. Then, as he got up to go, almost reaching the front door, the woman suddenly remembered something else. "One more thing, preacher, when they put me in that casket I want you to make sure they put a fork in my right hand. And when folks visiting at the funeral home ask about the fork I want you to tell them what it means. You see, I've been attending church dinners for years. And every time we have one of those church meals, when we get close to finishing our plate of food somebody will always say, "Now keep your fork. The best is yet to come!"

"Preacher, I want people to see that fork in my hand, in the casket, and I want them to know, for sure, the best is yet to come!"

I love and appreciate the gift of life. I enjoy living and having the opportunities which this life affords. Yet, as much as I love the here and now I am so excited about what God has planned for the then and there in eternity! For the Christian the very cool thing is that eternal life begins here and now (present) and never ever ends! Knowing that our future is so awesome and so secure in Jesus Christ enables us to make the very most of serving God and others in the here and now. Won't you join with me in celebrating and giving God thanks for the reality that THE BEST IS YET TO COME!

Scripture: Psalm 23; John 14:1-6.

Reflection: Those who have the greatest hope of heaven are most involved in this world.

Prayer: Giver of life, every moment is a gift from your hand. Thank you for the gift of earthly living. May we live each day as if it is our last – with gratitude and joy – that we may be prepared to die. So that living or dying we shall know with confidence that our souls are in your hands. In Christ our Redeemer we pray. Amen

8

Creation - Evolution Controversy

July 24, 2009

It seems to me sad, and wrong, that creationists bad mouth and discount evolutionists and that evolutionists bad mouth and discount creationists. Over the last 150 years (2009 marks the 150th anniversary of Darwin's "Origin of Species") each camp has been digging in their heels deeper and deeper.

This conflict and mutual disdain is even more senseless and tragic when we recall (in our better moments) that science and religion truly complement one another. Science and faith ask different questions. While science asks "how" faith asks "why". Science asks "when" and faith asks "who".

Creationists and evolutionists instead of self-righteously and condescendingly approaching each other would do well and benefit greatly from respecting one another's insights and opinions to one another's respective questions - how, when; and who, why. Science, and evolution as science, has so much to show us and inform us about God's awesome creation. Religion is necessary so that science is rightly and justly applied. Both are gifts from God. Both science and religion have so much to offer and contribute to human life and living. It is very possible to be a devout follower of Jesus Christ and also a supporter of the scientific method, including evolution. Instead of the creationist perspective to the far right; and, instead of the atheistic evolutionist to the left, there is another way that truly celebrates both God's involvement in the creation process (in the beginning and continuing) and the scientific method, including evolution. This way is called theistic evolution.

One of these theistic evolutionists is Francis Collins, head of the Human Genome Project. Francis intentionally reconciles his Christian faith with scientific theory, including evolution. In a recent interview with

Christianity Today in which Collins was questioned about his latest book entitled "The Language of God" he states: "One of the main reasons I wrote "The Language of God "was to try to put forward a comfortable synthesis of what science teaches us about the natural world and what faith teaches us about God. Yet it seems to be a well kept secret these days that the scientific approach and the spiritual approach are compatible. I think we've allowed for too long extreme voices to dominate the stage in a way that has led many people to assume that's all there is. The thesis of my book is that there is no need for this battle. In fact, it's a destructive battle. And we as a society would be well served to recover the happy middle ground where people have been for most of human history."

What should be our Christian take on evolution and how it relates to Christianity? How do you respond to the Collins' quote contained in the previous paragraph? What, in your opinion, should be the relationship between science and faith?

Scripture: Genesis 1.

Reflection: The Bible is not a science textbook, but rather a faith and love story.

Prayer: Creator God, what a majestic, glorious world you have made – the hues, the textures, the beauty, the variety – it is breath-taking and amazing! Thank you for the gift of science which helps us better understand the workings of your creation. Thank you for the gift of faith which enables us to be in relationship with you, our Creator. Amen

9

The Abortion Issue

July 31, 2009

Abortion is a complicated and divisive issue in America, in part because it strains the capacity of our culture and political system to discover a way to protect the life of the unborn in a society shaped by the value of individual rights and freedom. We Americans cherish the cultural value of being free to make our own decisions without interference from government.

Yet the freedom we exercise in the case of abortion is more than the liberty to live where we choose or to hold certain religious or political opinions we have adopted, since the exercise of this freedom results in the extermination of another human being.

The law of the land is not always a sufficient solution to personal moral and ethical responsibility. The United Methodist Social Principles affirm, "Governmental laws and regulations do not provide all the guidance required by the informed Christian conscience." Whatever the law might be, we human beings, and Christian human beings I might add, still have to exercise our own moral responsibilities as persons and develop together a culture that promotes and nurtures moral values and choices.

Scripture: Psalm 139.

Reflection: May we remember the sanctity of all life – the unborn and the born.

Prayer: Giver and Preserver of life may we recall the preciousness and sacredness of all human life. Let us never forget that every human being is created in your image. Herein the likeness of God is imputed and reflected in every person. May we work for the preservation and the restoration of life, seeking to practice and spread your justice and peace throughout the earth. O Lord, your kingdom come on earth as it is in heaven. Amen

10

The Topic of Homosexuality

AUGUST 14, 2009

One of my favorite ministry magazines arrived in the mail this week. I love to read through this resource because I find it such a great source of information and inspiration. One particular article grabbed my attention in this issue, probably because it was on the topic of homosexuality and I knew I would soon be preaching on this issue. The article is entitled, "Who's Your Leper?" The article asks, "Who is not welcome in your church? In your circle of friends? In your life at all?" It's tough to really answer these questions honestly. And if we are truthful the honest answers can be difficult to hear and process. There is a list of those who are shunned by some Christians and the list includes homosexuals, divorced people, the homeless, HIV/AIDS survivors, those with addictions, and many more.

As we read through the Gospel accounts we observe Jesus time and time again reaching out to the outcast and the downtrodden - those who are misfits and shunned from society.

The Pharisees - the religious leaders of Jesus' day - were horrified at Jesus' willingness to associate with those they considered untouchable. No one who was truly holy would even consider any form of contact with a woman who had ever been a "sinner" (Luke 7:37). Yet Jesus did not discourage such a woman from kissing his feet and rubbing them with her hair. And, rather than avoid lepers, Jesus willingly reached out to them with his loving, healing touch.

When it comes to the issue of homosexuality, or any other issue for that matter, how many of us act more like the Pharisees than like Jesus? Thanks be to God, Jesus does not look at us through a stereotypical lens or label. According to the scripture I read and the Jesus I know he looks upon each one of us as a child of God - - his child, created in the image of God and loved by God. Certainly there are sins of which the homosexual and the heterosexual need to repent. But let us not, fellow Christians, appoint ourselves as judge of another. Instead, let us reach out with love and acceptance in the same way God has demonstrated gracious acceptance and tolerance of you and me. I invite us, with the help of the Holy Spirit, to reflect honestly upon these questions as they apply to our life and living: Who is not welcome in our church? Who is not welcome in your life?

Scripture: John 4:1-30

Reflection: When Jesus comes into your heart he brings along all his friends!

Prayer: Lord, forgive our judgmental ways. When we are insecure it seems we are prone to put another person, or another group, down. Thank you that you are the judge and we are not. Rather than a self-righteous and judgmental posture to life, help us to be Christ-like – gracious and compassionate - in our approach to others, especially to the ostracized and oppressed. Amen

11

Singin' Methodists

AUGUST 28, 2009

It is customary for us at Oak Ridge UMC to have a "singing Sunday" every 5th Sunday. That is, we do a lot of extra singing during the worship services on these particular Sundays, and the sermon is in song (after some scripture reading we sing more hymns and songs). I think this provides a nice variety for our congregation and for all who attend and participate. In fact, many of us look forward to the 5th-Sunday-Singings so that we can spend additional time in musical praise to our Lord.

The early Methodists were known as "singin' Methodists. At worship services and camp meetings all over this land Methodists employed music and singing as a major component of any and all worship services. If we go back even further to England and John Wesley (founder of Methodism) we find that singing played a strong part in the Wesleyan spiritual movement. Indeed John's brother, Charles Wesley, authored more than 6,000 hymns!

John Wesley even had some "Rules for Singing" that were included in Wesley's "Select Hymns" Hymnbook published in 1761. Following is a sample of these rules for singing:

- Sing all. See that you join with the congregation as frequently as you can. Let not a slight degree of weakness or weariness hinder you. If it is a cross to you, take it up, and you find it a blessing.
- Sing lustily and with a good courage. Beware of singing as if you were half dead, or half asleep; but lift up your voice with strength. Be no more afraid of your voice now, nor more ashamed of its being heard, than when you sang the songs of Satan.
- Sing modestly. Do not bawl, so as to be heard above or distinct from the rest of the congregation, that you may not destroy the

harmony; but strive to unite your voices together, so as to make one clear melodious sound.

- Above all sing spiritually. Have an eye to God in every word you sing. Aim at pleasing him more than yourself, or any other creature. In order to do this attend strictly to the sense of what you sing, and see that your heart is not carried away with the sound, but offered to God continually; so that your singing be such as the Lord will approve here, and reward you when he cometh in the clouds of heaven.

May we sing unto our Lord with thanksgiving and praise every opportunity we have to do so. In fact, may our life be a song unto God. And, as we worship this weekend may we be reminded in the psalmist's words: "Make a joyful noise unto the Lord."

Scripture: Psalm 81:1; Psalm 95:1; Ephesians 5:19.

Reflection: Don't worry if you cannot carry a tune in a bucket, the Word instructs and invites us to "Make a joyful noise unto the Lord."

Prayer: O God, let us praise you and encourage one another through the gathering and singing together of hymns and praise songs unto you. May our songs of praise be a blessing to you! Amen

12

Work a Gift from God

SEPTEMBER 4, 2009

This Monday we observe Labor Day...a time to give God thanks for work and thanks for those who work faithfully and consistently to make this country and the world a better place in which to live. Let us also this Labor Day be mindful of those who are without work - those amidst the unemployed and underemployed ranks. We also pray that God will lend them strength and encouragement as they are in this waiting period of their life and living and that appropriate employment doors may open in a timely manner.

As scripture reminds us, work is a blessing, not a curse. Even though "work" is a four-letter word it is not at all a bad word or concept. In fact, contrary to some persons' thinking, work did not arrive on the human scene after the fall of humanity. Rather, work was a part of the divine blessing and assignment from the beginning: "God blessed them and told them, 'multiply and fill the earth and subdue it......tend the garden...'". Work, as God assigned it and designed it is meaningful, purposeful work. It is activity that responds positively to God's calling. In fact, the word "vocation" (a term we may also use appropriately for work) means "with voice" or "a calling." In this manner, work or vocation is that which God has called us to and equipped us for so that God's will may be done on earth as it is in heaven! What a difference when we see work as vocation - - as God's calling. In Ephesians we read these words concerning our work: "Work hard, but not just to please your employers when they are watching. As servants of Christ, do the will of God with all your heart. Work with enthusiasm, as though you were working for the Lord rather than for people. Remember that the Lord will reward each one of us for the good we do....." (Ephesians 6:6-8).

Let us give thanks on this Labor Day for all who work and may we recommit ourselves to work with faithfulness, enthusiasm and above all a sense of responding to God's calling (vocation). Perhaps the following prayer written by Reinhold Niebuhr might be ours at this season and time:

PRAYER: O God, you have bound us together in this life. Give us grace to understand how our lives depend on the courage, the industry, the honesty, and the integrity of all who labor. May we be mindful of their needs, grateful for their faithfulness, and faithful in our responsibilities to them; through Jesus Christ our Lord.

Scripture: Genesis 2:15; Ephesians 6:6-8.

Reflection: Contrast work as drudgery and work as vocation. What are some of the differences?

13

Remembering 9 - 11

SEPTEMBER 11, 2009

Today marks an unimaginable tragedy in our country. The mere mention of two numbers - 9 - 11 - and immediately everyone is on the same paragraph of the same page. No doubt we all remember where we were and what we were doing on that fatal morning. I was gathered with a group of community pastors for Tuesday morning Bible study at my friend Rudy's home. As soon as I returned from Bible study and walked into the church office I was informed of the diabolical terrorist acts. Members of our church staff gathered around a television set at the church watching in shock and disbelief as camera scenes showed unthinkable destruction, carnage and human suffering.

Of course our nation is different because of that day and because of that traumatic experience. There is a collective anxiety that was not there prior 9 - 11. Every time we go through security at an airport we are reminded. We see more weapon detectors where crowds are gathered for events; the presence of security personnel is more visible now; angst is more prevalent in our lives. The case could be made that we live in more fear as a result of this traumatic history - - we fear others more; our fear of the future is elevated; increased fear and anxiety has set up residence in our souls.

While we must be vigilant and prudent and wise in our life and living (Jesus tells us to "be as wise as serpents and as gentle as doves"), we need not become paranoid and filled with angst - the absence of peace in our hearts and lives. As followers of Jesus Christ we are gifted with a hope and a peace that shines through even (especially) in the darkest of times. While, as Christians, we are called to take practical and prudent measures so as to make good decisions and wise choices (whether in regards to potential terrorist acts or in our everyday life decisions), we are not to take on a worried, desperate, paranoid posture and attitude toward life. We are to be concerned, but not worried. We are not to stick our heads in the sand and cloister off from the realities of life; instead, we are to stay informed about, and stay involved in, the realities and needs of this world. Yet, we are to do so with the confident knowledge and assurance that "nothing can separate us from the love of God in Christ Jesus" (Romans 8). We are instructed in scripture: "Don't worry about anything; instead pray about everything......" (Philippians 4:6a). How about this statement for a fantastic Christian mantra?! Or, again, I Peter 5:7 reminds us, "Give all your worries and cares to God, for he cares about what happens to you."

We have an all-powerful and all-loving God who intimately cares for us and continually looks after us. We need not worry about today nor about the future for we are in God's hands. We need not carry around an anxiety-ridden spirit. Don't worry about anything; instead pray about everything. Trusting in God and his promises replaces worry in our hearts. Faith eradicates fear. Assurance trumps anxiety every time! Yes, remember. Yes, be vigilant, alert and wise. But, as a follower of Jesus Christ, never forget "Perfect love casts out fear!" And, in and through Jesus we are loved with a perfect, everlasting love. Praise be to God!

Scripture: Matthew 6:33-34; Philippians 4:6a; I Peter 5:7.

Reflection: We are called to be concerned but not worried. How do you define the difference? Worries and fears can easily consume us. 365 times the Bible tells us to "Fear not," or some form of this same message. Amazingly wonderful – one "Fear not" for each day of the year!

Prayer: You have promised, O Shepherd God, to be with us always. Even if we walk through the valley of darkness we are told to fear no evil for you are with us, your rod and staff they comfort and protect us. Enable us to not deny nor ignore our fears but to cast our fears and cares upon you for you care for us. Thank you that your love, perfect love, casts out fear. Amen

14

Radical, Christ-like Hospitality

SEPTEMBER 18, 2009

This weekend ORUMC begins a series based upon United Methodist Bishop Robert Schnase's book FIVE PRACTICES OF FRUITFUL CONGREGATIONS. Our topic this week is radical hospitality; or, as we at ORUMC call it, "Christ-like Hospitality." Radical, Christ-like hospitality is inviting, welcoming and caring for people in Jesus' name. It is offering a gracious welcome and showing acts of mercy to the stranger and guest because we have received the very same by Jesus Christ. People need to experience first-hand and see in action Jesus Christ in flesh and blood everyday reality before they will take a further step of trust into a Christian community. Radical, Christ-like hospitality offers an opportunity and responsibility for Christians to be Christ to the guest....to the stranger.... to the seeker. It invites another to begin the journey of faith with a specific community of believers, who realize and affirm that they have been so blessed to receive from Jesus undeserved mercy and grace that they cannot help but share this same welcoming grace.

Romans 15:7 encourages us this way: "Welcome one another, therefore, just as Christ has welcomed you, for the glory of God." Or, again, in Matthew's gospel (chapter 25) we hear Jesus saying, "I was a stranger and you welcomed me...." What a transformation should come to our welcoming, greeting, and practice of hospitality when we realize in welcoming another we are welcoming Jesus! Wow! That raises the bar for sure!

How are you practicing Christ-like radical hospitality? Do others see Jesus in how you greet and treat them? Do we really realize that when we welcome another person (stranger, guest, or friend) we are welcoming Christ? I pray that we will be more conscious of how we greet strangers (and each other) by remembering the radical hospitality that Christ has shown to us. And, I hope we, as Christians, will go out of our way to invite and welcome strangers and guests....remembering that the most simple and basic of kind gestures (friendly smile; a word of welcome; a handshake) can actually lead to an eternal difference in another's life and living!

Scripture: Exodus 22:21; Leviticus 19:34; Matthew 25:35; Romans 15:7.

Reflection: How are you showing Christ-like, radical hospitality to others?

Prayer: O Lord, once we were no people, but now we are your people. Once we were lost with no place to go, but you have taken us in. Help us to realize that in welcoming the stranger in our presence we are practicing and welcoming the presence of Christ.

15

Risk-taking mission and service

OCTOBER 9, 2009

We continue the series "Five Practices of Fruitful Congregations" this weekend with our topic this week being "Risk-Taking Mission and Service." Congregations and individual Christians that are vibrant and healthy engage not only in "in-reach" but also participate in outreach in Jesus' name. Like the Dead Sea - that only receives water and has no channel of outflow - churches and Christians spiritually die without engaging in outreach and service for Christ's sake.

The Old Testament prophet Micah tells us in his book that the Lord calls us to three things: Do Justice. Love Mercy. And, Walk Humbly with your God. That is a pretty good description of Christian mission and service. If we wish to bless the Lord, and avoid the "Dead Sea Syndrome", the pro-active mission and service formula is located in Micah's wise and ordained words. Through God's power and grace we reach out and become a channel of justice, mercy, and humility - - the waters of these qualities converging together to form a river of compassion and healing. First, the river flows to us from God's mercy and grace; and, then the river continues to flow in and through us to a world hurting and in need of God's healing mission and service. Let us reach out in mission and service by doing justice, loving mercy, and walking humbly with our God.

Scripture: Micah 6:6-8; Matthew 25:31-40; Acts 1:8.

Reflection: Both in-reach and outreach is necessary for a healthy, vibrant, and God-honoring life.

Prayer: Lord, in incarnation – God coming to earth and living in flesh – we have the motivation, power and model for mission outreach to the world. Not only does the world benefit from our loving service, but we require this for the life and health of our souls. May we do justice, love mercy, and walk humbly with you, O God. Amen

16

Extravagant Generosity

OCTOBER 16, 2009

This Sunday at ORUMC we wrap up a series entitled "Five Practices of Fruitful Congregations" by looking at EXTRAVAGANT GENEROSITY. In the Bible we are told about the poor widow who donated two pennies to the offering at the Temple. Just two cents! How could this be an account of extravagant generosity? Jesus tells us that because this poor woman gave from her heart - the right motive, which Jesus could see, and because she gave sacrificially (actually she gave all the money she had) she had given more extravagantly than the wealthy around her that day who had probably given hundreds of dollars!

It is not how much we give; but, instead how we give and how we give out of how much we have. The wealthy that day gave out of their abundance. They had plenty left over after they gave to the Temple work. The poor widow by faith put her last two pennies into the Temple treasury. She gave her all.

We may or may not be called and led to give all financially (although Christian stewardship calls us to remember that all we have belongs to God and should be used in a prudent and responsible manner), but we are all called as Christians to give from the heart - out of the proper motive which is love of God and others - and we are called to give sacrificially. Giving sacrificially out of love is practicing extravagant generosity. Can you recall a time you have practiced, or observed, extravagant generosity? A number of years ago I was part of a mission building team to the country of Haiti. Haiti is the poorest country in the Western Hemisphere. The average annual per capita income is around $500! We saw abject poverty and severe malnutrition all around us as we worked. I was privileged to mix mud and carry concrete blocks beside Tumah (a young Haitian man) all week long. We developed a relationship and communicated through the help of an interpreter located on the worksite. At the end of our days of working together, as we were preparing to share goodbyes with the local residents, our interpreter came up to me and said, "Tumah would like to say some words to you." And so we approached Tumah and he shared some words of appreciation and I reciprocated. And, then, he handed me a dozen eggs. Do you know what a dozen eggs mean in Haiti? It is for some Haitian families a couple days' worth of groceries! And he was presenting this gift to me as a sign of his appreciation for what we had experienced together on the worksite. That was extravagant generosity witnessed firsthand! And it has made a lasting impact upon me and I pray upon my wallet. May we practice extravagant generosity as we remember, and receive, what God through Christ has done for us....and given to us in the greatest gift in the world - the gift of Jesus Christ our Savior! And, as we give, and give generously, may we also be reminded that the act of giving is its own reward. We are never more like God than when we give. So, let's give of our time, talent, and treasures with generosity. As we have received extravagantly and generously, let us give with extravagant generosity.

Scripture: 2 Corinthians 8:1-14; 2 Corinthians 9:7.

Reflection: Created in the image of God we have an innate need to give.

Prayer: Giving and Generous God, you have given to us everything, including your only and holy Son, Jesus the Christ! All that we have comes from you. As we have generously and graciously received from you so may we generously give for your kingdom's sake. Amen

17

All Saints Sunday

OCTOBER 30, 2009

The writer of the Book of Hebrews (chapter 11) lists a litany of those who faithfully followed God - Abraham and Sarah; Moses, David, Rahab, etc. And, then, chapter 12 begins with these awesome words relaying a glorious truth: "Therefore, since we are surrounded by such a large crowd of witnesses to the life of faith, let us strip off every weight that slows us down, especially the sin that so easily hinders our progress. And let us run with endurance the race that God has set before us. We do this by keeping our eyes on Jesus, on whom our faith depends from start to finish."

This Sunday, November 1st, is All Saints Day. As followers of Jesus Christ we are assured of Jesus' presence and strength for this life, and we have the assurance of life with Jesus forever and ever! On All Saints Day we especially remember and give thanks for the lives of those saints (followers of Jesus) who have transitioned from the church militant to the church triumphant. During the processional hymn which begins our All Saints worship service (at ORUMC) we will once again sing these words: "For all the saints, who from their labors rest, who thee by faith before the world confessed, thy name, O Jesus, be forever blest, Alleluia, Alleluia!" ("For All the Saints" p. 711, United Methodist Hymnal).

Christians will gather to worship all over the world for All Saints Day. As they do so in the very midst of praising God they will also remember those who are no longer with us, yet who are part of that "large crowd of witnesses" cheering us on in the Christian journey. May we say a prayer of thanks to God, light a candle in memory, and name before God those saints who have been a part of our faith journey and who now "from their labors rest". Thanks be to God for all the saints!

Scripture: John 11:33-36.

Reflection: We grieve but not as those without hope. —St. Paul

Prayer: Jesus, we read that at the death of your good friend Lazarus you wept. Your heart grieved at his loss. We grieve over those whom we miss in our lives. Through the gift of good grief heal our hearts and through our grief journey may we come alongside others in their time of need and loss.

18

Big Time Encouragement!

NOVEMBER 13, 2009

It is always a blessing to be around a person who has the gift of encouragement. Persons who possess this God-given gift walk into a room and the mood brightens up. They have the unique ability to speak life-giving words! The words of affirmation they share can keep you going for days.

The word "encourage" in French literally means "to put the heart in," while to discourage is "to tear the heart out". Encouragers have a way of boosting your spirit and energizing your soul. So much in our world and in our culture is discouraging; so many messages seem aimed at tearing the heart out. But, the good news is God reaches out to us, supremely through Jesus Christ, to save us, empower us, and encourage us to live the abundant and eternal life He has called us to.

Hebrews 10:19-25 is one of those encouraging passages of scripture that "give us heart." The writer of Hebrews summarizes at the beginning of this short text how God, in Christ, has become our High Priest - the one who intercedes on our behalf so that our sins may be totally wiped out. What an awesome encouragement! Yet, the writer of this powerful scripture doesn't stop with us being encouraged. Instead, as we are encouraged so are we to encourage others. Hebrews 10: 23-25, for example, instructs us: "Without wavering, let us hold tightly to the hope we say we have, for God can be trusted to keep his promise. Think of ways to encourage one another to outbursts of love and good deeds. And let us not neglect our meeting together, as some people do, but encourage and warn each other, especially now that the day of his coming back again is drawing near."

May you and I be encouraged this very day by God's grace and through God's mercy. And, as we are encouraged by this divine graciousness may we share this encouragement with others for Christ's sake. Share a word(s) of encouragement with someone today.

Scripture: Ephesians 4:12; Hebrews 10:23-25.

Reflection: Who are you encouraging these days?

Prayer: God, you believed in us when we did not believe in ourselves. You see potential in each of us which we often do not see. You so loved us that you gave your Son. That is the ultimate encouragement!

19

Giving Thanks

NOVEMBER 18, 2009

As we approach Thanksgiving I encourage us all to take some intentional time to count our blessings and give thanks to God. In the words of an old gospel song, "Count your blessings name them one by one. Count your blessings see what God has done......". What a great idea! I suggest you take a pen or a keypad and list the many blessings in your life. You will be astonished by the results. Go ahead, carve out a block of time and start listing the long list of blessings, name them one by one. You may choose to start listing the blessings randomly. Others may choose a more guided approach. If so, below is a suggested partial list of categories.

The Psalmist proclaims: "Let us come before the Lord with thanksgiving" (Psalm 95:2a). Remember, this listing and recounting of blessings is not just for us, it is also to be a blessing unto God, for it blesses and pleases God when we acknowledge Him and thank Him for all He has done. So, when you make your list be certain to thank and praise God for all His wonderful gifts recounted on your list.

A suggested guided blessings list:

For the blessings of shelter, clothing, food, etc.
For the blessings of family and relationships - list by name
For the blessings of nature and animals - make a list of specifics
For the blessings of forgiveness when I fail.
For the blessings of sleep and rest when tired.
For the blessings of spiritual gifts, talents, and skills from God. List these in your life.
For the blessings of opportunities and options.
For the God-given spiritual gifts including: joy, peace, mercy, grace, and faith.

For the blessings of recreation and renewal.
For sabbath time.
Other blessings?

A THANKSGIVING PRAYER: We thank you, God, for blessings - The big ones and the small; your tender love and mercy that guards and keeps us all. The fresh awaking of joy that comes with morning light, sunlit hours to fill the day and restful sleep at night. The hope, the beauty and the love that brightens each day's living; we praise you, and our hearts are filled with joy, and with thanksgiving. We thank you for the fulfillment that's found in a job well done, the love of those who care, the peace of mind and serenity that comes with quiet prayer. In Christ name we thank you. Amen

Scripture: Psalm 95:2a; Colossians 3:15; I Thessalonians 5:18.

Reflection: Out of a heart of thanksgiving evolves gratitude and a generous spirit.

20

Let Souls Catch Up With Bodies

DECEMBER 4, 2009

The account is related about a group of American explorers who went to Africa, where they hired indigenous folk to be their guides. The first day they rushed through the jungle. And on the second day they were up at dawn, ready to push forward. And, likewise on the third, fourth, fifth, and sixth days.

On the seventh day, the American explorers were up again, anxious to get started. But they noticed that their guides were lying very quietly in their places of rest.

"Come on," shouted the Americans, "we are in a hurry!"

But the lead guide replied quietly in his broken English, "We no go today. We rest. Let souls catch up with bodies."

Advent is a season to wait, reflect and rest, in order to prepare for the greatest GIFT the world has ever received! Our tendency, however, is to move ever faster, doing more and more especially during this Advent-Christmas Season. How can we reflect upon the true meaning of this season without slowing down and reflecting? We cannot. How can we ever be ready for the arrival of the Christ child without intentional waiting and wondering? We can't.

This Advent, amidst all the shopping, partying, and going, may we carve out some time to let our souls catch up with our bodies. Not just rest (although that is a good and right thing) but rest with reflection, introspection and prayer.

Scripture: Isaiah 40:28-31; Luke 1:46-56.

Reflection: Spend some time this season in silence so that you may hear. Make the effort to empty some time on your calendar so that you may be filled with the things that truly matter.

Prayer: In our fast-paced, busy, and production-oriented culture, we do not like waiting one bit, Lord. Quiet our minds and still our souls that we may sit at your feet waiting for a word and listening for your voice.

21

Love that is True

JANUARY 22, 2010

We are fallen people living in a fallen world. Although we are created in our Maker's image, through original and personal sin that perfect image has been fractured and broken. God offers restoration through Jesus, yet we continue to stand in need of restoration and redemption. This is the meaning of "total depravity" as mentioned by theologians - - that every area and portion of our human life is affected by sin. Not, however, that there is no good within us, for the image of God is still present within us by God's amazing grace and gifting. But every aspect, every category of our life and living is scarred and negatively affected by sin. So, too, in our interpersonal relationships, even (possibly especially) with those whom we care for and love the most, our fickle and imperfect love shows through. Our love is limited at best; perverted at worst.

I was reminded of our conditional and fickle human love as I was out shopping in a local store one day this past week. And I came upon several aisles stocked with candy, cards and other items for Valentine's Day. Sayings like "Won't you be mine, valentine" and "Be mine, baby," and, "I love you, baby, be mine," appeared all over the products. And, while this is all fun and fine for this season, the love that is portrayed here is nothing unless it emanates out of God's unconditional love. For God's love is true love. God's love is not fickle and it is not based upon feelings. God's love is a covenant love, a commitment. You may neither earn this love nor merit this love. It is a free gift offered to all who willingly trust and believe God and God's promises. We learn about this agape, unconditional love of God primarily in the Gospels in the Bible, where we observe God's love first hand (in the flesh) in Jesus of Nazareth. We also learn what this love is like, for example, in the letter to the Corinthians (I Corinthians 13) when St. Paul provides fifteen qualities of God's agape love (verses 4-8). Some time ago I came across a resource entitled "The Love Test". It is a tool that can help us better understand God's love for us, and help us demonstrate that love more completely to someone we really care about. I suggest that you use this Love Test with a significant other in your life (a child, a parent, a close friend, a relative, a spouse). Each one take the "test", then compare your answers. This exercise has the potential of opening the door to some honest communication, and the potential of exposing some places where your love for one another needs to be fine-tuned with God's help.

I invite and encourage you to take the Love Test. Determine in your heart to love the way Christ wants you to love and will help you to love. Then, after taking the "test" perhaps you will place your completed test in a prominent place where you will be reminded daily of Christ-like love.

THE LOVE TEST (Based on I Corinthians 13:4-8) - Please read I Corinthians 13 prior to taking test (Rate yourself from 1 to 10 on each of the following characteristics of love with 1 being weakest and 10 being strongest).

1. I am tolerant toward and accepting of my significant other even when he or she displeases me (patient, verse 4) Rating _____
2. I am sensitive to my significant other's needs and endeavor to meet them even when I do not feel like doing it (kind, v. 4) Rating _____
3. I give my significant other "space" to develop his or her own potential and find his or her own fulfillment (is not jealous, v.4). Rating _____
4. I refrain from rehearsing my good points when my significant other is critical of me (does not brag, verse 4). Rating _____
5. I do not stubbornly insist that my way is best and demand that my significant other give in to me (is not arrogant, v4). Rating _____
6. I am considerate of my significant other's feelings and courteous in my actions toward him/her (does not act unbecomingly, v 5). Rating _____
7. I endeavor to look for my significant other's best interests as much as my own (does not seek its own, v. 5). Rating _____

8. I control my anger when my significant other displeases me (is not provoked, v. 5). Rating _____

9. I forgive and forget the wrongs my significant other commits against me (does not take into account a wrong suffered, v. 5). Rating _____

10. I do not take pleasure in my significant other's disappointments or failures (does not rejoice in unrighteousness, but rejoices with the truth, verse 6). Rating _____

11. I do not broadcast my significant other's faults in order to put him or her in a poor light (bears all things, v. 7). Rating _____

12. I endeavor to treat my significant other with absolute trust (believes all things, v 7). Rating _____

13. I look forward to our relationship growing more meaningful and precious (hopes all things, v 7). Rating _____

14. I do not allow our problems to rob me of my joy nor of my will to go on (endures all things, v. 7). Rating _____

15. I am totally and unconditionally committed to my significant other (love never fails, v. 8). Rating _____

TOTAL = _____

0-50 Improvement needed
1-100 Improvement desirable
101-150 Learning and growing; keep it up!

Scripture: I Corinthians 13

Reflection: Now there exists faith, hope, and love and the greatest of these is love.

Prayer: Loving God, not only do you show us love, you are love! Your love is the ultimate, supreme love – unconditional, agape love. Empower us to carry out your greatest commandment so that we would in doing so love you, love others, and love ourselves.

22

The Final Week of Jesus' Earthly Life

MARCH 24, 2010

What a week! Holy Week! Have you ever taken the time to reflect upon the events of Jesus' last week on earth? He stopped off at Bethany, the home of his good friends - Mary, Martha and Lazarus - for one last visit. Then, on Sunday, Jesus enters Jerusalem riding on a donkey as the crowds cheer and wave palm branches...a sign of military conquest. The crowds don't have a clue that they are cheering on the Prince of Peace, who has nothing to do with military battle.

On Monday Jesus clears the Temple as the money-changers have set up shop. Jesus will not tolerate this profaning of his sacred house of worship. On Tuesday Jesus spends some time teaching in the Temple and Jesus' authority is challenged and ridiculed.

On Thursday Jesus shares the Last Supper with his disciples....the Passover Meal becomes Holy Communion. The living bread and cup is literally before them. Jesus takes a basin and towel and washed the feet of his followers and he gives them a new commandment: "Love one another as I have loved you."

On the very next day, Good Friday as it is known, Jesus is tried by Jewish and Roman authorities in a ridiculous and unjust kangaroo court. At the same time Jesus is denied by one of his closest followers - Peter. And, at 9am on Friday Jesus is crucified. At 3PM his dead and battered body is taken down off the cross and Jesus is placed in a tomb.......

I encourage us to reflect upon what this Holy Week means in our life. Meditate upon the tremendous depth of God's love for humanity in and through His only and holy Son, Jesus the Christ. Try to absorb what happened during Jesus' last week on earth. What a difference a week can make!! What a difference was made eternally because of Jesus' last week on earth. The best is yet to come. Yet, we cannot get to Easter before Holy

Week. We cannot get to resurrection without crucifixion. Don't hurry by Holy Week and the Cross. Remember what Jesus endured and sacrificed on your and my behalf. What a week!

Scripture: Matthew 21.

Reflection: Jesus experienced every temptation and trial that we have ever faced and more. He understands. His final week on earth exemplifies this empathy and understanding.

Prayer: Jesus, your final week on this earth was filled with the full gamut of experiences and emotions – from celebrative entrance into the holy city of Jerusalem to being deserted by your followers and being crucified on a cross. You came, you served, and you died all for the sake of reconciling us to God through your loving and gracious sacrifice. May your name be praised above all others. Amen

23

Death of Dad

MAY 17, 2010

My Dad died three weeks ago today. I got the call from my brother a little past 6PM. He was gone. You are never ready for this call concerning the death of a loved one. I thought we'd have Pop for a number more years. After all, his Dad died at age 98 and his Mom died at age 95. We all just figured we'd have Dad into his 90s as well. But, it was not to be.

The loss is tough and the grief is deep. I have often preached from the pulpit that grief is a gift from God - - a God-given gift that enables us to heal. Now I am afforded the experience of "practicing what I preach." While I grieve Pop's loss, it is such a comfort to know he lived an active, vibrant life literally until he breathed his last breath. On the day he died he worked out at the heart rehab center; he "rescued" Mom at the local Wal-Mart parking lot, as she had gotten her car key stuck in the ignition and could not remove it. He was her knight in shining armor which gave him such pride; and, he picked up his granddaughter from school and brought her home; and, did some manuscript work in between. Not a bad day for an eighty-six year old man with heart disease who was to pass away a few hours later!

In all my nearly fifty-five years with Pop, every day was an adventure. Pop was a pioneer persona. He loved to investigate, explore and travel. He taught me so much about exploring life and setting and reaching goals. As his children, he always reminded us to keep our options open. But, while reminding us of options, he graciously and patiently stood back and allowed and encouraged us to make our own choices.

Most of all, in the midst of my grief, my heart rejoices because I know that Pop is singing in the heavenly choir. How Pop loved to sing! That was one of the main ways he worshiped. Singing was worship and therapy for Pop. At his Christian Service of Death and Resurrection I had the privilege of singing, with the help of my wife, Karen, and son Joshua and daughter, Anna, the song "Go Rest High on That Mountain." Later that same day we buried Dad's ashes in a mountain top cemetery which looks out over the land and the people he took care of and whom he dearly loved.

> *So go rest high upon that mountain, Dad your work on earth is done; Go to heaven a shouting; love for the Father and the Son.*
> *Pop, Go rest high on that mountain....the mountains and the people you loved and served, in the name of the Father, the Son, and the Holy Spirit. Amen.*

Scripture: I Corinthians 15:51-58.

Reflection: May we express our love and appreciation to our loved ones before they are gone.

Prayer: Lord, thank you for those we love and see no more. Thank you for the gift they were to us. Thank you for what they taught us living, serving, and loving. In your eternal name we pray. Amen

24

Blessed to be a Blessing

MAY 28, 2010

It's amazing the ability and power we have been given by our Creator with which to bless another! Very simple and every day acts and words have within them tremendous potential to bless.

Throughout the Judeo-Christian scriptures are found example after example where God affirms, empowers and blesses humanity - - - us!! As Father Abraham and Mother Sara, and many other followers since, have learned: We are blessed to be a blessing. The blessing that we receive is not intended to stop with us. The grace and affirmation that come our way is not to end there. The real beauty and the true joy of the blessing arrives as we are not only recipients of the blessing, but givers of the blessing as well.

For several weeks our congregation has been looking at and focusing upon The Biblical Blessing. John Trent and Gary Smalley, some years back, wrote a book titled The Blessing. This work traces the Hebrew, biblical blessing, illustrating that there are at least five (5) components to this blessing: 1. Words of affirmation; 2. Meaningful touch; 3. Envisioning a special future for the other; 4. Attaching high value to another; and, 5. Total commitment. To date, in our worship services and sermons, we have unpacked three (3) of these elements of The Biblical Blessing. During the month of June we will continue this series, as we seek to be people of God who are blessed to be a blessing. You will find this sermon series on the ORUMC website by clicking on the "sermons" link. Listen for the five (5) elements of The Biblical Blessing and see how you might practice these simple, yet powerful, steps so that your relationships might be deepened and strengthened. Several in our church family have shared some encouraging and inspiring stories of how they have intentionally practiced elements of the Blessing in their own relationships. How might you practice this blessing of another in your life?

Scripture: Genesis 48:8-16.

Reflection: Review the five (5) biblical blessing components listed above and evaluate how you are putting these supportive steps into practice in the lives of significant others in your life.

Prayer: O God, along with Abraham and Sarah, may we remember that we are blessed by you to be a blessing to others. Help us to be intentional and faithful about sharing the elements of the biblical blessing with the persons you have placed in our lives.

25

Lasting Liberty

JUNE 25, 2010

As we approach July 4th and Independence Day folks will, rightly so, be gathering and celebrating. As Americans we are incredibly blessed to experience the freedom we enjoy! May we give thanks for this privilege and never take it for granted. And, as we celebrate political freedom, may we as Christians, take this opportunity to cue us to think about, and give thanks for, an even greater freedom. It is a freedom that is not limited to any one land. It is a liberty that is not confined to any one people. It is the abundant and eternal freedom given through the grace of God by those who will receive. This gift of freedom in Jesus Christ is free but it is not cheap. It is offered without price, yet it cost Christ his very blood. This gift of Christ is given to us without cost yet, in return, if we truly accept and receive this gift, we will respond by giving all of our life.

Political and national freedom is a treasure not to be taken lightly. Having the freedoms of worship and assembly and even expressing our opinions in a blog, etc. are all precious privileges. Yet, as good and precious as these political freedoms are, there is nothing that compares with the spiritual freedom and liberty in and through Jesus Christ. Herein, we have our sins forgiven, our guilt removed, our life infused with purpose, the gift of the Holy Spirit to strengthen, comfort and guide us, with abundant life here and now, and eternal life forever and ever!

In the Book of Galatians, sometimes referred to as the "letter of liberty", Paul writes: "So Christ has really set us free. Now make sure that you stay free, and don't get tied up again in slavery to the law." Galatians is our charter of Christian freedom. We are not bound oppressively under the burden of law keeping. Instead, faith in Christ brings true freedom from sin and from the futile attempt to somehow be right with God by keeping rules and laws. We are free in Christ! Yet, as with any freedom, with it comes responsibility. Jesus sets us free to serve. He sets us free to follow his way of authentic love and true joy. May we not go back into slavery and oppression, but rather, follow the liberating way of God's love and grace, expressed and exemplified most completely in His Son, the Christ.

May we on this Independence Day, in the midst of giving thanks for our political freedom, be reminded of an even greater and eternal spiritual freedom that is free to us and to every man, woman, boy and girl on the face of this earth who will believe and receive. Happy Independence Day!

Scripture: Galatians chapter 5.

Reflection: True liberty comes with a life of responsibility and accountability to divinity and to humanity.

Prayer: Once we were no people, Lord, but now we are your people. Once we were trapped in our fears and bondage with no way out, but now we are set free through your grace and mercy. May we be ever reminded that this grace is not cheap grace, for it cost you everything – your very life on the cross for our sin. Freedom, whether spiritual or political, is never freely obtained, for it cost someone a great sacrifice in the end. May we give thanks each day for our freedoms and never take them for granted. Amen

26

Things we Treasure

JULY 16, 2010

The week before last Mom and my three siblings and I, along with our families, sorted through our deceased Dad's stuff. Pop passed away in late April, and Mom is moving in order to down-size since she no longer needs all that extra space and lawn to look after. I must say it was a chore. In some ways it was sad. It was not easy. And, yet, for me anyway, it provided further closure on Dad's death; and, it provided yet another cathartic experience. I was also blessed and impressed how sixteen of us could go about this difficult, emotional process and continue acting civil toward one another and come out still friends! I never heard one negative comment toward each other the whole three days of work. In fact, when it came to dividing up Pop's personal items there was only grace and graciousness expressed. Of course, as someone reflected, if we would of had one more day together "we might have witnessed a homicide!"

Dividing up Dad's personal items was difficult, but it has been very special to possess some of the material things that belonged to our Pop. In fact, as I write this blog I am wearing one of my Dad's shirts. I was also privileged to receive his beloved autoharp, which he often played and I sometimes accompanied him on guitar, a watch, and the family clock.... which the chiming conjures up many childhood memories. I know Jesus tells us to lay up treasures in heaven and not on earth, but in this case I believe these treasures are heaven-related, as they remind me of my Dad, who is in heaven with his Savior and Lord. It is not so much that these things are valued and treasured. Rather, they hold great value because they belonged to one whom I loved and respected deeply. They serve as a connector, a bridge, with Pop. This reminds me of a great spiritual truth I once heard. It goes something like this: There are only two things on this earth that are eternal - - the Word of God and the human soul. This is something to think about and something to guide our living and our priorities. What do we truly treasure?

Scripture: Matthew 6:19-34

Reflection: You can take all the material goods and possessions on this earth and pour them into your soul and your soul will continue to be empty.

Prayer: Giver of all life; Provider of all our needs, when our trust is in material things we miss out on the God-intended purpose of life – to love God and to love people. Help us to use things and love people, not the other way around. Help us to appreciate things as a means to serve you and with which to help others – resources to aid our journey together. In doing this we will not miss out on the meaning of life. Through Christ we pray. Amen

27

The Beatitude Attitudes

JULY 23, 2010

Our church family will soon be engaged in a church-wide study titled, "Life's Healing Choices." We will be reading John Baker's book by the same name, and with the subtitle: "Freedom from Your Hurts, Hang-Ups, and Habits." But, more importantly, we will be reading and reflecting during this series upon The Beatitudes, from Jesus' Sermon on the Mount. I am asking and encouraging all of us to read Matthew 5:1-12 each and every day August 1st through October 10th (The Beatitudes). What powerful and difficult teachings from Jesus!

The Oxford Dictionary defines "beatitude" with one word, "blessedness." Some dictionaries define blessedness as "happiness." One of the dangers of associating the beatitude teachings of Jesus with happiness is that it runs the risk of sounding too shallow and narrow in its meaning and description. The Beatitudes are never dependent upon circumstances and situations for happiness. Instead, practicing and living the Beatitude attitudes leads a person to a deep happiness - - - blessedness. One of the central philosophies and purposes of life and living for any person is this: We are blessed to be a blessing to God and to others. If we put into practice Jesus' words and instructions found in Matthew 5:3-12 we are on the road to healing and wholeness....and holiness. Through these attitude adjustment teachings we can truly take steps to find freedom from the hurts, hang-ups and habits that entangle and imprison.

Whether you are a part of our church family or not, I invite and encourage you to join the journey with us in covenanting to read Matthew 5:1-12 daily, August 1st through October 10th. Let's pray that God will use these readings and reflections to further bless us through healing us from our hurts, hang-up and bad habits, that we may make God-honoring, healthy choices, so that we may possess a "be- attitude" - - and be an even greater blessing to God and our neighbors.

Scripture: Matthew 5:1-12

Reflection: Look at each of the Beatitudes in Matthew's Gospel. In what ways is a person blessed by practicing these instructions?

Prayer: Lord, you have so much to teach us. And we have so much to learn! Your Beatitude teaching, from your Sermon on the Mount, seems so strange and contrary to common sense! How can being poor in spirit, meek, and persecuted result in happiness and being blessed? We have so far to go! Teach us Lord, and may we be willing students. In Jesus' name. Amen

28

Happy Birthday Aunt Jean

AUGUST 20, 2010

My wife Karen's Great Aunt Jean turns 106 today! Happy Birthday Aunt Jean! What a milestone! And, what a life! Jean made a career out of teaching school in the North Carolina Mountains, in the small southern town of Andrews. Former students relate that she was tough and she was fair. They also relate that you never....ever....wore a cap into her class. That spelled big trouble! So, a few years back some of us guys in the family purchased some customized ball caps with big letters on the front which read, "AUNT JEAN'S HAT," which we all wore into her house that day. After getting a playful chewing out...she laughed and thought it was hilarious.

Jean jokingly attributes her longevity to never being married. She stated to me not long ago that she "didn't have a man to bring her down." I have been privileged to know Jean for 30 years. Observing her life I have been inspired and instructed. She not only has obtained quantity of life, but she also has lived a quality life. As I think about Aunt Jean on this her 106th birthday I reflect upon some of the many qualities in her life that have enabled her to live a long and a good life...they include:

- A great sense of humor. Jean never took life nor herself too seriously. This reminds me of the wise philosophy which teaches - - Take yourself less seriously; take God and his ways more seriously.
- An incredibly open mind. Aunt Jean has seen SO many changes in her lifetime. It reminds me of Tofler's "Future Shock." Yet, Jean has remained a person who "bends so that she will not break." She has an amazing mind for her age. And, she has an amazingly open mind for her age. As someone has truthfully stated, "A closed mind is like a closed parachute." The result is a hard fall!

- A deep, abiding faith in Jesus Christ as Lord and Savior. Jean speaks naturally about her Savior and supports this verbal affirmation with a Christian lifestyle.
- A great love for Lance crackers. When you ask Jean about her favorite snack she will say, "I love Lance crackers." Karen and I think that Lance Crackers has missed an incredible opportunity for a very effective advertisement campaign for their product. Imagine having a 106 year old lady in the mountains of North Carolina...saying, "I have enjoyed Lance crackers ever since they started making their product. A pack of Lance crackers a day keeps the doctor away!" Well maybe not, but Aunt Jean, at 106 years of age, I think you should have a pack of Lance crackers on us today....and any day you wish! Happy birthday Aunt Jean!

Scripture: Psalm 71:9; Isaiah 46:4; Luke 2:36.

Reflection: Thanks to God for those who go before us, showing us the way. May those older in age know and be recipients of our appreciation and respect.

Prayer: O Lord, we thank you for those who though older in chronological years, yet display an open mind and a positive spirit. We are encouraged by those who rather than becoming rigid and calloused in their perspective, evidence and practice a flexible posture toward life. Keep us appreciative and pliable so that we may bend and not break. For Christ's sake. Amen

29

The Family that Plays Together, Stays Together

AUGUST 27, 2010

The statement "The family that plays together, stays together," may not be true 100% of the time, but the practice of this philosophy sure can improve the unity, cohesiveness, and fun for a family and a relationship with a significant other. I grew up in a family in which we often played games. Almost no day went by where we didn't play something--Sorry, Life, Monopoly, Candy Land, checkers, Chinese checkers, backgammon, chess, ping pong, shuffle board....and the list continues. What fun times! And, what great memories! Games provided a way to relate, de-stress, except when I was losing, and just have crazy fun times.

I spoke by phone with my Mom last evening. She became a widow this past April. I've asked her several times how she's adjusting. One of the things she mentions is how lonely it is in the evening hours. She stated that she missed Dad so much for many reasons, but one of those reasons is that she and Dad had a game time almost each and every evening. It was part of their routine. They'd sit around the kitchen table and play word games, or Skip-Bo, or Rummikub, or something. She shared that she missed that connecting time so much.

I'm alone this weekend. Karen went to be with her mother who recently had a fall and needed some extra help. I miss Karen for a lot of reasons, but one of those reasons includes the fact that we will not be continuing our Rummikub "tournament" for a few nights. Almost every night we now find ourselves seated around our kitchen table for a rousing game. It's really not so much the game....although Karen would tell you that I keep score with paper and pen each game!! (Of course - you have to have a winner or it's not a game!!). But, truly, if I'm truthful it's about connecting time. When Karen and I play Rummikub, for example, we do strategize our game....but, I find it is much more about chit-chatting and laughing and playing footsies under the table. Games are such a great way to relate, unwind and connect with those you love.

I recommend that you turn off the T.V., put down that newspaper, and get out a game and have some connecting time. It will be fun...and you will create some lasting positive memories.

Scripture: I Corinthians 10:31

Reflection: What are some ways that you enjoy your significant others relationships and nurture these relationships even further? In what ways do you participate in leisure and play together?

Prayer: Lord, thank you for the people that you have placed in our lives. Help us to make time and take time to nurture and cultivate our relationships. May we treasure the moments we have with these folks. May we not only pray together, but may we engage in healthy play together. In Jesus' name we pray and play. Amen

30

We Can't Do This!

OCTOBER 8, 2010

I was tired. It felt like the weight of the world was on my shoulders. I was mired in a pity party. I had taken so much responsibility - - we call this "over-functioning" in the therapy world - - that I had left God's grace out of the equation! How short-sighted! How presumptuous! How wrong!

As one of the pastors at our church, involved in the planning and administration of our current capital campaign, I had developed a myopic ministry mode! I had gotten bogged down in the details and fierce and fast pace of the campaign and I had left out the most essential....until someone stated the truth...and the truth (as it always will, provided we heed it) set me free. This person, commenting in relation to our church's campaign stated: "We can't do this." He had our attention...then after he paused for effect he then went on to say, "We can't do this, but with God's help and guidance we can!" It was like a ton of bricks had been lifted off my shoulders! Because of one person's faith and wisdom, manifest through a brief statement, I now have a proper perspective restored. I now have a peace about this. I now have a renewed faith that we as a congregation, with God's help, can indeed accomplish this vision which God has planted within us! Wow! How quickly we can develop a small faith and a blinded vision! This smallness of faith reminds me of the guy that sold small sharks. He stated that folks loved to purchase his small sharks for their home aquariums, and other habitats. He went on to say as long as you keep these sharks in relatively small containers the sharks remain small. However, if you put these same 6-inch sharks into their natural habitat (the ocean, etc.) they grow to be many feet in size. That's the same way with Christians. As long as we stay in our own small circle....in our own small thinking.... in our own limited faith-perspective...we remain small, baby Christians. But, when we have a God-sized, fiercely God-dependent faith....we grow so that we may have a greater impact for God's kingdom. And, the weight is lifted off our too-small shoulders....putting the focus back where it should be: upon God and his sovereignty and glory!

Scripture: Jeremiah 29:10-12; Matthew 11:28-30.

Reflection: Scripture instructs, "I can do all things through Christ who strengthens me," not "I can do all things."

Prayer: God, we can easily become over-extended and overwhelmed. We pretend that we can handle anything that comes our way. We highly value and exalt independence and self-sufficiency. Yet, fierce independence and undue self-reliance leaves us empty, depleted and often defeated. Help us to recognize our need for, and consistently practice, reliance upon you. Amen

31

College Basketball, Professional Football and Christian Financial Stewardship

NOVEMBER 5, 2010

November to me means a time of year when my favorite sport begins....
college basketball. I love the fast-paced, acrobatic athletic movements, and
the strategies of a closely contested game of b-ball! November also means I
have the luxury of viewing my second favorite sport - - professional football.
After a wonderful and jam-packed Sunday morning of leading worship,
mingling with God's people, and preaching 3 sermons at 3 worship services
I am ready to go crash in my lazy boy and watch some football (of course
a little food is in order prior to crashing!).

As a Christian, and as a Christian pastor, November has also
traditionally signaled the soon to arrive financial stewardship Commitment
and Pledge Sunday at local churches. I am grateful that our congregation
talks about Christian Stewardship throughout the year (prayers, presence,
gifts, service, and witness - - on a regular, round-the-calendar basis), but
we still have our COMMITMENT SUNDAY when we offer to God
our financial support for the next year's MINISTRY INVESTMENT
PLAN (Budget), to further celebrate and solidify our dedication in making
followers of Jesus Christ.

I have so much to learn about Christian financial stewardship. There
is so much further I have to go. But, I was blessed to learn about financial
stewardship from my parents. Not so much that they talked it...but
they modeled it. I saw their commitment to the church we attended. I
witnessed their regular support of the missions and ministries. I viewed
their generosity to the church...with their time, presence, spiritual gifts and
financial contributions. My parents' attitude was not "We have to do this
giving." Rather, it was "We get to do this." Scripture tells us, "God loves a
cheerful giver." That does not mean giving, financially for instance, is easy.

It does not mean it will not be a sacrifice...sometimes it will require this. But, it does mean that when Christian financial stewardship is Christian.... it will happen out of a love response to God.....out of falling in love with Jesus...more exciting and meaningful than either professional football or college basketball! Authentic Christian financial stewardship gives to God cheerfully, consistently, regularly, and out of first priority. That is, the one who is in love with God does not give God left -overs, but instead first fruits. This is one important way of reminding ourselves and signaling to others that God has first place in your life and living. Then, as a result, this giving is not a haphazard, random giving ("O, well, I'll just throw a $20 dollar bill in the offering today...that's all I've got."); Instead, it is intentional, planned, and prioritized, and done out of a response to God's incredible love for, and gift to, us ultimately in Jesus Christ his only Son! I am amazed how we will, without thinking, give a 15 - 20% tip to a person who serves us a meal; yet, we will not give 10% to the One who has given us everything, including our very life.

I pray that this year, and every year, we will enjoy the wonderful opportunities and activities life has to offer (possibly college basketball and professional football, or other choices)....and the great and joyful privilege of practicing the spiritual discipline of generous financial giving to Christ's church.

Scripture: 2 Corinthians 8.

Reflection: When it comes to financially giving to God's Kingdom work, would you be considered more a haphazard tipper or a consistent tither?

Prayer: Lord, forgive us when we give you leftovers rather than first fruits! If you are truly number one in our lives then it will show in the commitment and giving of our time, talents, and treasures, which are all graciously loaned to us from you for a time. Help us to grasp that we do not have to give, we get to give! In Christ we pray. Amen

32

Making Room for the Best

DECEMBER 10, 2010

It's so easy to get caught up, and swept away, in a life that is overly filled and too busy, especially, ironically at this time of year....A time of year, named Advent on the Christian calendar. Advent: a time in which we are invited and encouraged to spend time waiting and pondering and watching. Advent: a season to gain proper perspective. Advent: a time to make room for the best things in life. So often we fill our lives with things (possessions, events, busyness, work) not bad things, and even good things. Yet, because of our full plate we do not take time to include the very best of life and living. The result: An unfed hunger and continual thirst in our souls, which long for something more...something lasting. The very thing which we need for soul care is that for which we have no room. No room...plate full!

In Luke's Gospel we read, "And while Joseph and Mary were in Bethlehem the time came for her baby to be born. She gave birth to her first child, a son. She wrapped him snuggly in strips of cloth and laid him in a manger, because there was no room for them in the village inn." No room for Jesus who had come to this world. That was the human response that night long ago, and it continues to often be our response to Jesus today - - No room!

And, yet, Jesus still knocks on our heart's door...seeking entrance, hoping for time and attention, offering love and grace. And to those who receive Him they are called his daughters and sons. May we open our hearts and lives to the Christ child, to our savior Jesus. Interestingly, we were created HUMAN BEINGS, not HUMAN DOINGS. When we get so caught up in the doing - - the activity, the performance, the busyness - - we can lose our proper focus and our lives become un-centered and unbalanced. Like a good potter who centers clay upon the potter's wheel, our lives need centering upon the ONE who wishes to shape us and transform us into a work of beauty and grace --a life reflecting God's love and mercy and light to a dark and merciless world. May you and I take some time this Advent-Christmas Season to be still and silent before God... to reflect upon our BEING made in the image of God; to take some time for BEING with Jesus so that our doing may be transformed. Take some time to make room for the very best.

Scripture: Luke 2:1-7; John 1:10-12.

Reflection: How are you currently making room for Jesus in your life?

Prayer: Hymn of prayer – "Come into my heart. Come into my heart. Come into my heart, Lord Jesus. Come in today. Come in to stay. Come into my heart, Lord Jesus." Amen

33

Entering a New Year

JANUARY 14, 2011

As we continue to navigate into the early part of 2011, an idea that I recently heard on the radio seems worthy of passing on. I was out running, headphones on, recently when the Christian radio personality to whom I was listening shared the idea that instead of making, and breaking, a New Year resolution, how about adopting a particular word or phrase. This word or phrase which you choose becomes your vision for this New Year. It could be an area in your life that needs addressing or improving. It could be a goal or focus for this year. Perhaps it would be a part of your life which needs strengthening.

Hearing this, and continuing to run, I did some reviewing of my life. What would be a word or phrase that, I prayed, God would give me, to claim for 2011? After some reflection the phrase MERCIFUL OUTREACH came to me. The more I contemplated this phrase for my life the more I knew it was so appropriate. Merciful = Showing loving kindness. And, Outreach = Reaching out to others beyond our comfort zone. So, reaching out beyond my comfort zone to demonstrate the loving kindness of Jesus to others...this, I hope and pray, will be my focus and emphasis for this New Year and beyond.

I encourage you to consider selecting a word or phrase that will serve as your emphasis and concentration for this year. Possibly pray that God would lead you to this word. Maybe you would spend some time meditating upon what area(s) of your life need some attention and strengthening so that God would be glorified. May you, with God's help, find a word or phrase that will guide and direct your path in a positive direction throughout the coming year.

Scripture: Psalm 119:11.

Reflection: Focusing and meditating upon the Word of God and words from God serve to keep our lives centered in God's will and way.

Prayer: The Jesus Prayer has been prayed by many followers of Christ throughout the ages. It provides a centering focus which can serve to guide and heal. Suggestion: Pray this brief, yet powerful, prayer over and over when you feel stressed, when you cannot sleep, when you are longing for a heightened awareness of the presence of Jesus. "O Lord, Jesus Christ, Son of God, have mercy on me a sinner." Amen

34

Healthy Relationship Practices

FEBRUARY 12, 2011

A lot is said and shared this time of year (February and Valentine's Day) about love and relationships, so I figured I would add my own two cents. When I think about healthy relationships and the work that a healthy, nurturing relationship requires, I often think about my Dad's reflections and advice concerning this topic. Dad passed away April 26th, 2010 after forty-seven years of practicing medicine as a Family Practitioner. He had a passion for a more general practice of medicine - i.e. Family Practice, etc. - in part because he was an advocate for holistic treatment, affirming the interrelatedness of body, mind and soul. Aware of my work as a part time marriage and family therapist, Dad would sometimes share with me about his work with couples (especially pre-marital couples) whom he sometimes counseled at his clinic. He told me that he would present to them the "3-C's" of a nurturing, positive relationship. I find them to be very helpful, straight-forward, and full of common sense, although common sense isn't always so common in these times in which we live.

Here are Dad's 3-C's:

Commitment: Any relationship which hopes to be strong and secure needs trust. This is the bedrock of any healthy and nurturing relationship. When a person knows that the other person will be with them through the ups and downs; through good times and bad times...whatever comes their way....this breeds a security that enables and empowers a love to not only grow, but to blossom, in all its fullness.

Communication: There is poor communication and there is positive communication. We communicate ALL the time, no matter what we are doing or saying. Here we are speaking, of course, of positive communication. Positive communication consists of two general headings and practices: Active listening and assertive sharing. In active listening we not only hear physically (with our ears) but we also seek to listen emotionally (with our heart), that is, we seek to understand what the other person's words and body language are saying. To do this we ask a lot of questions. We inquire of the other person for clarification and explanation, staying focused upon them and their sharing....NOT our agenda. You might try a simple (but difficult) exercise for active listening to another. Listen to someone share for a few minutes and then repeat back to them what you heard them saying. This is a great way to stay focused upon their words and their thoughts and feelings. If you truly practice this you will not be focused upon your thoughts and what you will say in response to their words. Then there is assertive sharing in order to practice healthy communication. Assertive sharing is telling the other person that for what you wish. It is expressing your true feelings and thoughts and wishes to another in a non-threatening, non-demanding style. And, it can avoid a lot of passive-aggressiveness in a relationship, because you are telling it like it is, instead of hiding feelings and thoughts. Active listening and assertive sharing are two essentials of positive, healthy communication in a relationship.

"Complimentation": Everyone needs and desires to know that they are valued and appreciated by significant others in their life. Sharing compliments, whether pertaining to another's physical, mental or emotional attributes and qualities, goes a long way in nurturing and strengthening a relationship. Here I would add another quality with a play on words. Both "COMPLIMENTATION" and COMPLEMENTATION are necessary for a growing, functional relationship. While complimentation involves words and expressions of valuing and appreciating another, complementation includes affirmation of, and realizing the need for, variety in a relationship. The strongest of relationships complement one another, where each person recognizes they have strengths and weaknesses and that they help balance and support one another when they complement each other.

So, these are Pop's 3'C's, which I find worthy of passing on...and, I hope you find them helpful in all your relationships. Growing and nurturing healthy relationships is not easy. There is required work. But I believe, along with Dad, that commitment, communication and "complimentation" and complementation can provide the tools and the framework that is needed for good, strong relationships.

Scripture: Ephesians 4:15-16.

Reflection: Rare, but beautiful, is the person who practices both sharing the truth and relating that truth in love. We can probably recall many times when someone shared the truth but in a not so loving manner. And, we also remember, no doubt, someone sharing information in a kind and caring way, but without being real and totally honest.

Prayer: O Lord, positive, growing relationships require time and work. May we carve out the time, and give our undivided attention especially to those dearest us. Through genuine compliments and attentive communication (active listening and assertive sharing) may we exemplify strong commitment in our relationships. In the name of our Triune God – Father, Son, and Holy Spirit – who exemplifies for us, and empowers us for, life-giving relationship. Amen

35

Solitude, Silence and a To-Do List

MARCH 21, 2011

The Season of Lent invites us to come clean before God. I find that in order to do this necessary "house-cleaning" of the soul it is good and right to carve out some intentional time for reflection and introspection with Holy Spirit guidance. Genuine introspection will lead us to honest confession which, in turn, leads to a liberating of the weighted soul.

While I am aware that my soul requires this reflection time, there is a problem: I am a type-A personality. Folks like us, in the interest of time attempt to multi-task. We have been known, for example, to brush our teeth, read the newspaper and go to the rest room simultaneously! We have things to do and the world to change. Who is going to "tend the store" if we are away or if we aren't vigilant? So, we continue to ignore and avoid "sabbath time." Authentic sabbath time, which facilitates and fosters solitude and silence, gets displaced and abused by too-busy people. We end up caught up in a noisy exterior and a noisy interior....even our alone thoughts are fast-paced and loud!

It requires purposefulness and personal discipline to step off the treadmill in order to reflect and renew. But the results of taking and making the time to do so are like fresh air to the lungs! As a person and as a pastor, I know that I need to come apart before I come apart. I have finally learned through my mind thick and dull (and with the help of some good spiritual guides) that if I do not spend some regular and extended periodic time with God in solitude and silence, then I am not equipped nor prepared to share with nor lead the people God has placed within my pastoral care. The under shepherd must be nurtured and led by the Good Shepherd. You must be fed in order to have something with which to feed others.

This week I will again take a mini-spiritual retreat...to come apart so that I do not come apart. It will be a spiritual and a physical challenge for me, once again, to practice solitude and silence. Even though part of me resists these spiritual disciplines, my soul craves this time. And, as a type-A personality, I will once again spend the first portion of this personal "retreat" working my to-do list (getting it, hopefully, out of my neurotic system) -- engaging in this "human doing" stuff, so that I may spend the final portion in the therapeutic, nurturing time of just being before and with my Creator...so that I may be re-created for God's plans and purposes.

May our Lenten journey include times of solitude and silence in which we may hear and heed the still small voice of God.

Scripture: Psalm 46:10; Matthew 6:5-6; Mark 1:35.

Reflection: Come apart before you come apart!

Prayer: Jesus, you who are God, while on this earth you protected your time alone with the Heavenly Father. In scripture we read over and over how you went away alone, or with your disciples, to spend time in intentional prayer and reflection. If you, as God's Son, needed and craved that communion and alone time with God, how much more do we require this spiritual manna so that we may have something to give to others. In the name of the Bread of Life we feast and pray. Amen

36

An Easter Sunrise Memory

APRIL 22, 2011

I called Mom last night. Each Thursday evening I usually do this. Each of us siblings takes a different evening to call Mom, ever since Dad died last year. During our conversation, amongst other topics, Mom and I reminisced about our many Easter sunrise services attended as a family through the years. Some of our favorite services were those hosted on top of Long Meadow. Long Meadow Mountain is just as its name suggests - - - a long meadow on top of a mountain, almost 5,000 feet in elevation. Members of our small country chapel would drive up to this meadow early on Easter morning in time to watch the breath-taking sunrise from high atop the mountain meadow. What an awesome vantage point for an incredible sunrise view!

As an early teen I recall one Long Meadow sunrise in particular. As we were gathered on the ridge in the early morning darkness, just prior to dawn, watching the beginning of the sunrise, suddenly a jet plane and its long vapor jet stream appeared on the horizon. What a contrast! Divinity's sun was rising in the east, while at the same time humanity's invention was soaring across the sky in front of our view of the sunrise. Humanity seeking to interrupt Easter sunrise! And, yet, the jet along with its vapor exhaust soon disappeared and dissipated but the sun remained high and strong in the skies. Easter would not be stopped. Sunrise was not to be long interrupted. May you and I be reminded and assured this Easter and always: Easter will not be stopped. "Son" rise will not be interrupted! Have a blessed Easter!

Scripture: Mark 16.

Reflection: Because of Easter we have an endless hope instead of a hopeless end!

Prayer: Risen Lord, on Easter morning God's power raised you from the dead! The grave and death's sting could not hold you down! Now, through a faith and trust in the resurrected Christ Jesus, we are Easter people. We have eternal life beginning here and now and never ending! Alleluia! Amen

37

Festival of the Christian Home Month

MAY 6, 2011

This time of year we often think family....Mother's Day (May); Father's Day (June) and Festival of the Christian Home Month (May). Family is that place where "iron sharpens iron." It is not always easy. Sometimes being family is downright tough. Yet, if we allow and do our fair share in terms of responsibility and participation family can be a pretty special and cool deal. And in that specialness we are being shaped and formed for life and living. I often quote American poet Robert Frost's line which says, "Home is the place that when you go there they have to take you in." Why? They must take you in because that is where you belong. This is the way it should be. This is the way it is intended to be. My heart and compassion go out to those houses where it is not truly a home and where dwellers therein do not really perceive and feel that they do belong!

It takes work. It takes commitment. And, above all it takes unconditional love to make a functional family (as some have quipped dysfunction is a relative matter - - pun intended!) and a wholesome home. Proverbs 24:3-4 tells us: "By wisdom a house is built, and by understanding it is established; and by knowledge the rooms are filled with all precious and pleasant riches."

Following are some wise words for building a healthy home from writer Dorothy Nolte. They apply to all God's children, big and small -

If a child lives with criticism, he learns to condemn.
If a child lives with hostility, she learns to fight.
If a child lives with ridicule, he learns to be shy.
If a child lives with shame, she learns to feel guilty.
If a child lives with tolerance, he learns to be patient.
If a child lives with encouragement, she learns confidence.

If a child lives with praise, he learns to appreciate.

If a child lives with fairness, she learns justice.

If a child lives with security, he learns to have faith.

If a child lives with approval, she learns to like herself.

If a child lives with acceptance and friendship, he learns to find love in the world.

May our families and homes be places of nurture and healthy relationships so that we may reach out and make the world a better place in which to live. Take and make some time to nurture your family!

Scripture: Proverbs 24:3-4; Ephesians 5:31-33; 6:1-4.

Reflection: "Home is the place that when you go there they have to take you in." - Robert Frost. What does this quote from Frost mean to you?

Prayer: Heavenly Parent, thank you that in you we live and move and have our being, for in you we have a home and there it is we belong. Through your Son, the Christ, you have assured us that we have our residence in you, for Jesus tells us, "Remain in me, and I will remain in you." Help us know that place of rest and residence in you, O Lord, our Help and our Home. Amen

38

The Freedom of Grace

JULY 1, 2011

On this Independence Day weekend I give thanks for the opportunity and privilege of living in a land with so many freedoms. There are many on this globe not able to enjoy these same liberties. May our prayers go out to them, especially those who are living under totalitarian and oppressive governments and rulers. May we also remember and show our gratitude to those who stand in harm's way so that we may be the recipients of such great freedoms.

I believe and affirm that our Creator God created all human beings to be free....free from oppression; free from inhumane ways....and, freed for shalom - - a wonderful and rich Hebrew word filled with God's pro-active peace consisting of, not just the absence of war and conflict, but filled with the justice and mercy of a loving God.

This is where our deepest and best freedom comes from.....God's shalom! God frees us from our sin and from our self. We humans are broken and self-centered and sin-ridden...hubris (or selfish pride) eats away at even our best laid plans, thoughts and actions. Yet God in and through Jesus Christ makes a way to restore us; a way to set us free; a path by which to truly liberate us. Romans 3:24 celebrates: "By the free gift of God's grace all are put right with him through Christ Jesus, who sets them free."

We on the Wesleyan Branch of Christianity are a movement which celebrates and emphasizes God's grace......amazing grace! We often speak in United Methodist circles of God's same grace manifest in at least three manners: Prevenient Grace; Justifying Grace; and, Sanctifying Grace. We cannot escape God and his grace. It is all around us. It surrounds us. It invites us. It woos us. It even protects us. This is God's prevenient grace. The grace that seeks us out. The grace that convicts us. The grace that first loves us...so that we may even respond to and love God.

While Prevenient Grace does not require a human response, Justifying Grace does. In Justifying Grace we admit our need of God. We agree with God that we cannot solve our sin and self-centered problem. As we admit and confess our need of God and God's grace, God offers us reconciliation...salvation......redemption. We no longer attempt to be self-sufficient. We no longer try to prove ourselves. We rest in God's amazing, forgiving, healing justifying grace. What liberty! What freedom!

While Justifying Grace frees us from our self and from our sinful ways, sanctifying grace frees us to walk the Christian journey. Sanctifying Grace is a shared project with God in which we accept God's guidance for our life and living. It is living our life so as to look more and more like Jesus. As one Wesleyan theologian puts it, prevenient grace speaks to us as barely human; justifying grace as truly human; and, sanctifying grace as fully human.

God is offering us total and complete freedom both now and forever! As we give thanks for our temporal national freedom may it remind us of a deeper, permanent, and universal freedom in and through Jesus Christ.

Scripture: Romans 3:24; Galatians 4:31 – 5:1.

Reflection: Look up the words Prevenient, Justifying and Sanctifying. What do these words mean to you in terms of God's grace?

Prayer: Loving God, before we could reach out to you, you reached out to us. Before we were lost and defeated in our brokenness, but now through your amazing grace, through you Son's sacrificial gift on the cross, we are made whole. Before we had no purpose, we were wandering directionless. Yet, now you are continually making us more and more into your likeness. Thank you for your undeserved, amazing grace! In Jesus' name we pray. Amen

39

30th Wedding Anniversary

AUGUST 26, 2011

This week my wife, Karen, and I observed and celebrated our 30th wedding anniversary. I am incredibly blessed to have such a loving and giving and patient spouse! In some ways these past 30 years have seemed to fly by. In other respects, when I reflect upon all the experiences and life journeys that Karen and I have encountered together....hey, it adds up to a lot!

One thing I am reminded of as I reflect upon thirty years of marriage.....a strong, lasting relationship (of any sort) takes a lot of time, investment, patience and nurture. In fact, I Corinthians, chapter 13, often referred to as "The Love Chapter" when describing love begins this way: "Love is patient; love is kind...." Whenever I read these characteristics of love, along with the fourteen additional descriptors of true love, I get convicted. How often in my 30 years of marriage have I not practiced patience! How many times did I not engage in kindness! And so the relationship inventory goes on and on. Ah, but then I read (I Corinthians 13:5b) true love "keeps no records of wrong," and I am given renewed enthusiasm and hope for my marital relationship (and any other relationship)! Forgiveness! Grace! Mercy! When we've received it from our Creator we then can share it with others...and with our significant other!

I am so grateful that Karen is a grace-filled person...she would have to be to be married to me! I am thankful that she does not keep a record of my wrongs done against her. And, I also want to reciprocate and practice that same grace toward her. Yes, a lot of patience....a big dose of kindness and a ton of forgiveness....from God and from one another......has enabled us to reach thirty years together and counting! It is a gift. This relationship I count as a treasure. And to Karen is awarded The Purple Heart Award for sticking it out...lo these thirty years. Of course, she has no choice. I have told her on more than one occasion, "Karen, if you ever leave me...I'm going with you!"

Scripture: Colossians 3:12-19.

Reflection: A strong relationship is like "iron sharpening iron." What is your response to this statement?

Prayer: Lord, thank you for your incredible patience with us! And, thank you for those in our lives who are patient with us. May we also practice kindness and patience with others. In our Lord's name. Amen

40

When Ordinary Becomes Extraordinary

SEPTEMBER 23, 2011

We can so easily miss out on seizing the moment because we are either looking back at yesterday or anticipating tomorrow. Sometimes we seem to be living on cruise control and not really absorbing nor realizing the beauty of the here-and-now. In this fog and funk we begin to refer to life as mundane, ho-hum, and ordinary.

Not long ago my wife Karen and I reflected upon this "ordinary" trap that can so easily snare all of us human beings. We had several folks in our congregation who were going through serious health and medical trials and treatments. We discussed how these particular folks would simply long for and treasure a so-called ordinary day! How their lives had changed from one day to the next when they received these medical diagnoses. Suddenly, ordinary day became a longing.

Earlier this month I experienced a wild and chaotic day. I took our daughter, Anna, to the college campus she attends for her classes. As we drove onto the school grounds a policeman flagged us down, telling us to vacate the premises because the college had received a bomb threat. Later that same day we experienced an earthquake. Our church staff was seated around a conference table as the earth shook! Then, that evening a hurricane hit our Eastern coastline. A bomb scare; an earthquake; and, a hurricane...all in the very same day, in the same state! I wondered what would be next! I was thinking I should be alert for the locusts to come ravaging! I can surely tell you that I welcomed ordinary after that wildly eventful day!

May we truly have our eyes open to the gift and beauty of each day! May we recognize the special opportunity that every moment of each day offers. And, in doing so may we see and seize the extraordinariness of ordinary days. Seize the day...right now! Don't wait for tomorrow or some day.

Leo Buscaglia shares (submitted by one of his students):

Remember the day I borrowed your band new car and I dented it? I thought you'd kill me, but you didn't. And remember the time I dragged you to the beach, and you said it would rain, and it did? I thought you'd say, "I told you so." But you didn't. Do you remember the time I flirted with all the guys to make you jealous, and you were? I thought you'd leave me, but you didn't. Do you remember the time I spilled strawberry pie all over your car rug? I thought you'd hit me, but you didn't. And remember the time I forgot to tell you the dance was formal and you showed up in jeans? I thought you'd drop me, but you didn't. Yes, there were lots of things you didn't do. But you put up with me, and you loved me, and you protected me. There were lots of things I wanted to make up to you when you returned from Viet Nam. But you didn't.

May all your days be extraordinary!

Scripture: Ephesians 5:15-21.

Reflection: In our home while growing up a framed cross stitch on our den wall read, "Only one life will soon be past. Only what's done for Christ will last."

Prayer: O Living God, forgive us when we are the walking dead – merely existing from one moment to the next, not truly living. May our minds and hearts be open to your grace and guidance and may our eyes be open to see the beauty of your world in the smallest of miracles and wonders! O Lord we pray. Amen

41

Gratitude Generated Generosity

NOVEMBER 11, 2011

I will always remember with great fondness a former church member of mine by the name of Paul. Paul was filled with gratitude. His signature statement was, "It's great to be alive!" And he truly LIVED each and every day. And, I remind myself, his life was not always easy. Toward the last part and season of his life his wife, Bea, had Alzheimers disease. He kept Bea at home with him as long as he possibly could. But there arrived the fateful and dreaded day when he had to place his mate of more than 60 years into a skilled care facility. That was an enormously difficult day! With tears in his eyes and a positive faith, Paul made the trek and carried out the gut-wrenching but necessary action.

For years Paul made the trip from home to nursing home, twice each day, to feed Bea her meals and to lovingly speak to her and to comb her long, silver hair. He would often speak words of love and encouragement to Bea as he stroked her hair lovingly with his hand; saying words like: "Bea, I'm so glad God gave you to me!" "You are the love of my life!" "It's great to be alive and to be here with you!" And the times that I was privileged to enter into this sacred space with two faith-filled and positive personalities I was encouraged and inspired! Often at these visits with Paul and Bea, after visiting and sharing together and after a word of prayer, Paul would hand me an offering envelope for our church, which contained his tithes and offerings to help enable and sustain ministry, frequently saying: "Pastor, God has been good to me and Bea. Life is a blessing! It's great to be alive! Please take this offering to the church." Gratitude seeped from Paul! Thanksgiving and gratitude continually generated his generosity in every aspect of his life.

Scripture: I Chronicles 29:9; Proverbs 3:9; 2 Corinthians 9:7.

Reflection: Created in the image of God, we have an innate need to give.

Prayer: Gracious God, may we recall the sacredness and the gift of each moment in time. So let us treasure each day and each relationship we have been given so that we may respond with grateful and generous hearts. In Christ we pray. Amen

42

In Advent Awaiting Freedom

DECEMBER 16, 2011

One winter season our family had an unwanted and a surprise guest in our house. A mallard duck somehow made her way into our chimney but could find no passage of escape! The contour of the chimney made exiting impossible and the glass covering the fireplace opening prevented exiting in that direction....thankfully for the home dwellers! One early morning Karen and I were abruptly awakened by a horrible racket seemingly coming from our living room. As we got up and further inspected, we noticed a fowl in our fireplace! So, what to do?! We finally came up with a plan. Karen would open the glass covering while I would move in with a blanket and capture the bird. It worked! I grabbed the mallard, which was exhausted by this time with lack of food and water coupled with repeated efforts at "prison-breaking," and took her to our front porch. As I opened the blanket she spread her wings and headed in flight toward a nearby lake. Finally she was free. At last she was liberated. Yet, without outside intervention she would never have made it.

As we wait this Advent Season....waiting for Christmas, and more specifically waiting for the arrival of Christ, may we be reminded that we, imprisoned in our addictions and idolatries, and self-centeredness cannot liberate ourselves. Jesus comes to set us free! God, thankfully and graciously, invades our world and our egos in order that we might be liberated and rescued! This is the joyous anticipation of Advent! May we ever remember that even in the very center of waiting and wondering.... Jesus...Immanuel....God with us....Savior of the world....is coming to our world....to live in our hearts....to rescue us from sin and self....to set us free! As I remember and reflect upon the beauty of the mallard taking flight after being freed, I am given a picture, an image that deeply encourages my soul! Our deliverer is coming! Help is on the way!

Scripture: Romans 7:15 – 8:6. Notice the contrast between Romans chapter 7 and Romans chapter 8.

Reflection: "There is no condemnation for those who are in Christ Jesus…" Romans 8:1a.

Prayer: Liberating Lord, we long to be freed – freed from our sin, freed from our idols, freed from our addictions. We follow our own ways and wishes and ironically this path leads to a soul imprisoned. We become so filled with self that there exists no room for you. God, empty us of self so that you may fill us and in the process we shall be freed. Thank you, Lord. Amen

43

Our Small Individual Worlds

JANUARY 30, 2012

Our human condition lends itself to staying in comfort zones. We like the familiar. We don't handle change too well. I am a creature of routine. Perhaps we all are. But those of us who rate high "J" on the Myers-Briggs Temperament Profile have a high propensity to structure, routine and closure. Closure and things like written lists give us a sense of control in life (pseudo though it may be). If I am to be spontaneous, and open to change, then I will write "be spontaneous" on my list.

One of the inevitable downsides to being overly structured and unwilling to shake routine, thereby attempting to avoid change, is that it stunts growth. No stretch, no growth. No resistance, no strengthening. Gail Godwin writes, "There are two kinds of people...one kind, you can tell just by looking at them at what point they congealed into their final selves. It might be a nice (enough) self, but you know you can expect no more surprises from it. Whereas the other kind, keep moving, changing... they are fluid. They keep moving forward and making new trysts with life, and the motion of it keeps them young. In my opinion, they are the only people who are still alive. You must be constantly on your guard... against congealing."

This congealing can happen to us if we do not purposely step out of our boats and out of our comfort zones. May we stay open to new learnings and new possibilities so that we may grow for the kingdom's sake.

Scripture: Isaiah 40:28-31; Philippians 3:12-15.

Reflection: Old 4H motto – "If you're green you're growing. If you're ripe you're rotting."

Prayer: Creator God, we are designed and wired to grow. When we shrink wrap our world, please forgive. When we fail to step out of the boat at your call, grant mercy. For your Kingdom's sake let us soar like eagles; let us run the race with all we've got. In your name Lord. Amen

44

Haiti Trip

FEBRUARY 12, 2012

Tomorrow morning a mission team from our church leaves for the country of Haiti. I am so honored and excited to be among this group! This will be my third trip to this Caribbean country. The first time I was a thirteen-year-old lad going with my Dad (a medical doctor) on a medical mission team. We travelled to Cap Haitian on the northern coast of Haiti. I recall as a young boy watching the Haitian folks, some who had walked all day, arriving to get in line so that they and their children might be treated for various medical conditions. I also recall the patience practiced as they waited in a long line for long hours to finally maybe be seen. I contrasted this with a trip to the grocery store, for example, in my American home town....and, how we folks can't wait a few minutes in an express lane without getting impatient and sometimes irate. What lessons in patience I learned from these wonderful and poverty-stricken people!

My second trip to Haiti came when I was thirty-two years of age. My wife, Karen, and I, along with a church mission team worked alongside some Haitian folk to help construct a residence for a nurse. We worked each day on the worksite mixing cement, carrying concrete blocks, and forming walls. Each evening and on Sunday morning we would gather in a simple, stark and small building which was their church. The first time we entered we noticed a placard or sign in a corner of this sanctuary. Upon asking what this was we were told it was a fund-raiser campaign for a church organ. They were hoping and praying to find an organ for their services of gathered worship. There are many things that I would think of providing for a people who are extremely poor and often physically hungry but I must say an electronic organ is not one of them. Yet, this was a desire of their hearts. They placed a great deal of emphasis and importance upon worship of God, and specifically worship in song and praise. I could not help but think of the biblical account in which Jesus willingly and openly received the gift of the expensive ointment poured upon his feet and some of his followers commented that this money could be used to care for the poor. When we returned home to the United States from our mission trip several of our church members began a financial campaign to raise money for a sanctuary organ for this congregation in Haiti. Over six thousand dollars was raised in a matter of a couple weeks. These monies were sent to the congregation in Haiti and they got their church organ!

These Haitian accounts, and many other Haiti stories, have been planted in my psyche and heart since I was a young teen. I have often reflected upon what life lessons God has taught me through the Haitian people. Now, early tomorrow morning I head to Haiti for a third journey to that land. I know God will have so much more to teach me through the people of Haiti.....if only my eyes and my heart are open! O Lord, may it be so.

Scripture: Luke 21:1-4.

Reflection: Why is it that those who materially have the most in this world often seem to give the least, and the "least of these" seem to frequently give much out of their little?

Prayer: Lord of all, to whom much is given, much is required. We have been taught that we are blessed to be a blessing, yet our read is that we somehow deserve what we possess; that it is all ours to do as we wish. So often the poor and the disenfranchised teach us much about giving and about generosity! Perhaps because they have so little to lose they become liberated to give, whereas we in wealthy places become so bound by our stuff and possessions that true liberty is missed. Lord forgive. Amen

45

Haiti Continued

MARCH 9, 2012

When my life is out of alignment and I need to regain proper perspective it is amazing how God resets my spiritual compass to true North through service, outreach or being sent on a mission to serve others! Our culture and our human condition combine to attempt to move us further away from what is good and right and needed. We insulate ourselves. We pile layer and layer of protections and things between us and vulnerability and dependency. We like to consider ourselves as self- sufficient. We aim to be in control. Yet, the irony is that the person who considers themselves to be in control is, in truth, out of control.

Recently I spent nine days in Haiti with a mission team. Ever wonder why we call ourselves a "Mission Team"? Actually, we should probably call it something like "Missioned to Team." Because that is what inevitably occurs. You go with a mindset to be in mission to others and you end up being missioned unto! I never want to glamorize nor patronize the poor and poverty. Poverty is horrible and demeaning. But, there is something within the poor (and the broken and the handicapped, for that matter) that is close to the surface - - hand-to-mouth; day-to-day. And, therefore, I affirm and observe that they in many ways are closer to God...or, at least, more aware of their dependency (including dependency upon God). Perhaps this is why Jesus declares, "God has anointed me to preach good news to the poor."

The poor, the broken, the handicap have much to teach us. Perhaps the greatest lesson they teach us is that we are also poor and broken and handicapped. For, unless we see this about ourselves we are indeed blind. Henri Nouwen put it this way: "The suffering person calls us to become aware of our own suffering."

How can I respond to someone's loneliness unless I am in touch with my own experience of loneliness? How can I be close to handicapped people when I refuse to acknowledge my own handicaps? How can I be with the poor when I am unwilling to confess my own poverty?

When my life is out of alignment.... when I need to regain proper perspective.....God seems to speak to me the loudest and clearest when I am willing to engage in outreach and service in Jesus' name.

Scripture: Isaiah 61:1-3; Luke 3:16-21.

Reflection: "Blessed are the poor in spirit; for theirs' is the kingdom of heaven." Matthew 5:3

Prayer: Holy God, we are all broken people. As your Word reminds us, all have wandered and gone astray. The truth is we need to be broken before we can be made whole. We resist being called terms like broken, incomplete, even fallen, but the reality is that when we face the truth and own it, it frees us. What a heavy, burdensome and impossible weight to carry around – the image that we are complete and whole! That is too much for anyone to carry! For only God can carry your weight and my weight and the weight of the whole world. As we sometimes sing out to You, Lord, "He's got the whole world in His hands." Thank you for carrying us when we can no longer carry ourselves. Amen

46

Good Friday

APRIL 6, 2012

Because of the torture, persecution, mocking and violent death on the cross that Jesus endured for all humankind, it is sometimes with ambiguity that I employ the term "Good Friday"! That first, and original, Good Friday would have, no doubt, been anything but good....certainly for Jesus' followers. Their hope was gone. Their joy was absent. Because Jesus was gone....dead and buried! In fact, Jesus' followers were so disturbed and frightened that only one attended the crucifixion. The others fled for their lives out of fear. Nothing "good" about death and dying and tombs and tears!

And, yet, there miraculously was! Jesus dying was our ticket to life! Death on a cross wiped out our sin as a victor for good! As the prophet of God proclaimed, "By his stripes we are healed!" Pre-resurrection Good Friday was not good. But, praise be to God, the grave could not contain Jesus! In Christ life conquered death! And, now, truly.....every Good Friday since has been GOOD!

Scripture: Genesis 50:20; Mark 15:22-34; Romans 8:28; I Corinthians 1:18.

Reflection: Only God could take something bad and tragic and transform it into triumph and good!

Prayer: God, you seem to specialize in making something good out of that which seems so bad. Lord, through your power and grace, transform our lives that we may be a part of the transformation of your world. In Jesus' name. Amen

47

Family Matters

MAY 4, 2012

This month we observe and celebrate Festival of the Christian Home and Mother's Day amidst additional celebrations. I visited with my soon-to-be eighty-seven-year-old Mother just last week. It happened to be during the second anniversary of Dad's death. We were able to share some of our sadness and emote some of our grief. I continue to be amazed at my Mom's amazing physical energy and mental sharpness! And, I continue to be grateful for God's gift of a godly and loving Mother!

Among the many lessons and gifts that Mom has taught me (and many other folks) are these -

SACRIFICIAL LOVE: I recall the many times that Mom sacrificed so that I, or my siblings, could benefit. For example, she purchased clothing for us and got herself none. Or again, the many trips out of town (giving up time, energy and financial resources) for all of us siblings so that we could have braces on our teeth - which she needed but never was able to receive. On a daily basis she prepared meals, worked in our family garden, washed tons of laundry, taxied us to events and activities, cleaned house, some years in addition to employment outside the home....and still took time to console us, read to us, and attend to a plethora of needs and concerns.

SIMPLICITY: Mom had been raised in a family considered by many as relatively poor and; in addition, reared during the depression years. She had learned the way of hard work, little financial pay, and carefully saving - - wasting nothing. These attributes and methods carried over into her adult and family life. She appeared to have the gift of making "something out of nothing." She could certainly take a little and make it stretch. She taught me, and our family, the lesson of simple beauty. More really can sometimes be less. Clutter and over-abundance and obsession with material things can rob persons of perspective, freedom and joy.

SERVING: At almost eighty-seven years of age, Mom, during most weeks hauls meals-on-wheels to shut-ins four days in the Appalachian Mountains which she calls home! From serving her Lord and church, to serving her family, to serving her community and neighbors, serving has always been a lifestyle - - a way of life - - for Mom.

Happy Mothers' Day 2012 Mom! Thank you for the lessons I have received through you! But, most of all thank you for being my loving Mom!

Reflection and Action: Perhaps all of us during this month which observes Celebration of the Home and Mothers' Day would take some time to reflect upon and give thanks for those qualities we have received and learned from our family members. Maybe you would be led to complete (or begin) a family map - - a genogram (websites are available to inform and instruct on this valuable family tool). All of the above, and more, could lead to a renewed and stronger appreciation for your family and family members.

Scripture: 2 Timothy 1:1-7

Prayer: Thank you, O Lord, for the family members who have been a blessing in our lives – those who have taught us in both word and deed, and those who continue to teach us, the path of righteousness. Amen

48

Father's Day Reflections

JUNE 15, 2012

My Dad died a little over two years ago. I don't think a day goes by that I don't think about him. I am so privileged to have some of my Dad's diaries and a Grandparent's Reflection Journal that our children and I gave to him in which to make entries. I reviewed some of these diary entries just this week and they took me down memory lane. Precious memories! Memories in my Dad's hand writing. Memories like the family games we used to play; the mountain hikes Dad and I would often take; the Brutal 100 bike ride he and I took one year; the times as a young boy I would go with my Dad to make house calls in the Appalachian hills; and the father-son mission trip we took to Haiti.

Dad was one who taught much more by his lifestyle and actions than by his words. With him, more was caught than verbally taught. I was blessed to have a Dad who taught me integrity, a good work ethic, a love for God's creation, and the values of faith, family and a pioneer spirit that wasn't afraid to step outside the box. As I went through some of Dad's writings I once again read what I have come to label "Pop's Principles for Living". They are -

- "Whatsoever thy hand findeth to do, do it with all thy might." Ecclesiastes 9:10
- "In all thy ways acknowledge him, and he shall direct thy paths." Proverbs 3:6
- And, Changes come but one anchor endures: A life built upon the person of Jesus Christ.

Happy Father's Day to All!

Scripture: Deuteronomy 6:7; Colossians 3:21.

Reflection: Thank God for fathers who seek to be men of integrity – not perfect, but authentic.

Prayer: Heavenly Father, thank you for our dads. Like us, they are not perfect, but probably have done the best they can with what they have and what they have experienced. One of the beautiful promises from you, O Lord, is that you pledge to be a father to the fatherless and to those whose fathers are less than they should be. Parent us, and re-parent us if need be, so that we may share your goodness and mercy with others. In the name of the Father, the Son, and the Holy Spirit. Amen

49

The Lord's Prayer

JULY 13, 2012

Our congregation is currently engaged in a series of worship services and sermons focusing upon the model prayer Jesus gave to his earliest disciples - - and to us - - known as The Lord's Prayer. Perhaps it would be better to call it The Disciples' Prayer since the prayer is not for Jesus, but for Jesus' followers.

I have prayed this prayer since I was a small child. We prayed it in our little mountain chapel every Sunday morning. And I have prayed it with fellow worshippers in various settings and contexts - from outdoor youth retreats to local church sanctuaries to a cathedral in the holy city of Jerusalem. It is a universal prayer for all people and all times.

It has been good and right to focus more closely upon this marvelous summary prayer. One aspect of this prayer which truly amazes me is its brevity yet comprehensiveness. I timed myself praying this prayer in an unhurried manner. It took all of 30 seconds! 30 seconds in which to say it all! Many times we think of prayer as adoration of God, and The Lord's Prayer does include that reality of prayer (Our Father in heaven hallowed be your name); but, the bulk of the prayer is petition. Jesus is instructing us, asking us, to pray seven (7) petitions. We are invited and requested to pray for: God's name (Hallowed by your name); God's kingdom (Your kingdom come); and, God's will (Your will be done on earth as it is in heaven). God is first because, well, God is first!

Next, we are invited and encouraged to pray four more petitions. And the fourth petition is located at the heart - the center - of the Prayer. When we stop and think about this - the petition for daily bread - why is this petition in the prayer at all? In the very center, having just prayed for God's name, kingdom and will, Jesus places the petition for our every day, ordinary, flesh and blood request - daily bread! Yes, God, our heavenly

Parent cares greatly about his children's everyday physical needs. God is interested not only in "soul salvation" but also in "whole salvation." In addition, this asking God for daily bread reminds us over and over of our total dependency upon God - - which is no small thing for all people and possibly especially no small thing for those of us who are steeped in a culture of materialism and saturated with restaurant and food choices! Reminder: In the final analysis and outcome we have nothing without God's provision! "Give us this day our daily bread," reminds us of God's gracious and generous provision and of our dependency upon the generosity of God.

Finally, in the last three petitions of The Lord's Prayer, Jesus instructs us to pray concerning: trespasses, temptations, and avoidance of evil. It is all right there in one brief, but powerful, prayer! In a 30-second prayer we pray a prayer of adoration of God; prayers for our needs and the needs of others - both physical and spiritual. We pray for the past - Forgive us our trespasses; we pray for the present - Give us this day our daily bread; and we pray for the future - Lead us not into temptation. The Prayer even includes each member of the Holy Trinity: God (Our Father in heaven); Jesus Christ (Forgive us our trespasses....); and Holy Spirit (Deliver us from evil). The more I consider this prayer the more I see. I now have a renewed appreciation for this disciples' prayer and a renewed love for Jesus who graciously provided us with this all-encompassing prayer!

Scripture: Matthew 6:7-15.

Reflection: The Lord's Prayer is the disciples' prayer.

Prayer: Our Father, who art in heaven. Hallowed be Thy name. Thy kingdom come, Thy will be done on earth as it is in heaven. Give us this day our daily bread and forgive us our trespasses as we forgive those who trespass against us. Lead us not into temptation but deliver us from evil for thine is the kingdom, and the power, and the glory forever. Amen

50

Not Trying, but Training

AUGUST 17, 2012

I greatly enjoyed watching the Olympic Games recently. I specifically admired the awesome athletic talent and courage on display. For example, the young American female gymnast, winning her first gold medal; or the double amputee from South Africa competing in relay races; and, an American relay runner finishing his portion of the race on a broken leg! What courage and perseverance on display!

It occurred to me while watching these amazing athletes perform, that they do not just show up in London, England and TRY for the Olympic events. Rather, they TRAIN for these games. They are tested and disciplined on a regular and consistent basis over and over long before their arrival in London.

I think there is a lesson here for our Christian journey as well. The strength and perseverance for our Christ-following path does not come by simply trying or through just trying harder. Overcoming and moving forward happens through our trust in God, relying and depending upon God's power and resources....trusting to the point of training.

To the Christians in Corinth St. Paul pens these words: "All athletes practice strict self-control. They do it to win a prize that will fade away, but we do it for an eternal prize." Or, again, in I Timothy 4 we read: "Spend your time and energy in training yourself for spiritual fitness. Physical exercise has some value, but spiritual exercise is much more important, for it promises a reward in both this life and the next."

When we observe Jesus' own life, for instance in the wilderness temptation experience, we see that Jesus overcame evil and Satan through the use of spiritual disciplines - silence, solitude, scripture and prayer. Jesus kept in touch with God. He made this communication the priority in his life regularly...consistently. He did not just TRY to overcome the enemy; rather, he TRAINED through connecting with his Heavenly Father.

This is the secret to moving forward and finishing the race well.

Scripture: I Corinthians 9:24-27; Philippians 3:12-14.

Reflection: O God, the life of truly following Christ is not the life of least resistance! In fact, the road is at times very difficult. Through your grace, diligence, and our God-given will power may we consistently and faithfully train for the race you have set before us. Through your power, O Lord, may we run and not be weary. In Jesus name we pray. Amen

51

Emotionally Healthy Spirituality

SEPTEMBER 21, 2012

During a recent Sunday morning sermon I invited each hearer of the message to consider ONE of the following "Ten Symptoms of Emotionally Unhealthy Spirituality." While each one of us could certainly benefit from improvement and growth in each of these ten areas, perhaps there is ONE area of the ten that is more pressing for us right now in this season of our life. Here are those ten areas -

1. Using God to run from God. Your prayers are basically my will be done, not God's will. This involves hiding behind "God talk." We know and we speak the right lingo and rhetoric, but we continue going our own way.

2. I ignore the emotions of anger, sadness and fear. I don't consider how God may be coming to me through those emotions. We often minimize, or even deny, these very real feelings and emotions rather than honestly processing them. The faith community has sometimes been guilty of setting unreal and unhealthy "rules," such as "We don't get angry around the church as good church members." How unfair and how untrue! Where two or more are gathered there will exist anger at some point and time. In fact, the Bible instructs, "Be angry and sin not." Anger is not the problem. Rather, it is how we deal with our anger that is the issue.

3. I'm dying to the wrong things. We are intended and created to enjoy and to share the good gifts of life -- gifts such as joy, art, music, beauty, recreation, laughter and nature. Some folks, unfortunately, feel guilty unwrapping those presents from God. Christians are NOT baptized in lemon juice.

4. You are denying the past's impact on the present. You have not looked at some of the issues and patterns of your family of origin and your culture and how this impacts and influences you today.

5. Dividing your life into secular and sacred compartments. You have a spiritual life right now in church. You have work and recreation, for example, in another compartment.

6. You are doing for God instead of being with God. This is about not developing your personal relationship with God. Serving God has become a drudgery on automatic pilot rather than a relationship of joy. Someone once noted, "We are created human beings, not human doings."

7. Spiritualizing away conflict. The belief that smoothing over disagreements or "sweeping them under the rug" is to follow Jesus continues to be one of the most destructive myths alive in the church today. Much like anger, spoken about earlier, conflict is not the problem; rather it is how we deal with conflict that becomes the topic to address. Rather than avoiding conflict those who practice emotionally healthy spirituality embrace and deal directly and timely with conflict.

8. Covering over brokenness, weakness, and failure. Trying for a certain spiritual image instead of being real before God and before others becomes the goal. May we remember that none of us is perfect...in fact far from it. The ground is level at the foot of the cross. We are called to be real. Not pretenders.

9. You live without limits, instead of being obedient to God-given boundaries. We need to do SOMETHING but we cannot do EVERYTHING. We are not God. We cannot serve everyone in need. Jesus did not heal every sick person in Palestine. He did not raise every dead person. He did not feed all the hungry beggars. Jesus often got away to be alone with God and with his disciples. We need to take care of self so that we may be enabled and strengthened to care for others. An everyday example of this comes from the airlines. Whenever a person flies on a commercial airliner a flight attendant will instruct the passengers that in the event of an emergency oxygen masks will be made available. The instruction is given to make certain you place the oxygen mask

on yourself before helping a child, elderly, or other person place a similar mask up on themselves. The reason? So that the helper has sufficient oxygen and strength to thereby help another in need. The caregiver must take care of self so that he or she has something to offer another in need.

10. You judge the spiritual journeys of other people. Usually this is a sign of your own lack of emotionally healthy spirituality and the need to put someone down so that you might look better.

May we each take inventory! These ten statements, while not exhaustive, provide a fairly comprehensive overview of our emotional and spiritual life. Perhaps you and I would consider ONE of these ten and pray that God would bring healing and health to this particular area so that we may better reflect and relate the Light of the world in our daily living.

Scripture: Matthew 22:37-40; Colossians 3:17.

Reflection: God created us as whole beings – body, mind, and soul. How are we giving attention to and nurturing each and all of these areas?

Prayer: Healing God, our lives can so quickly become unbalanced. You have created us as whole, integrated beings. Each part and aspect has impact upon the other. At times our souls are depleted and our minds cannot think clearly because we have not taken adequate rest. Help us to value and to care for every part of our God-created and God-loved being. May we strive for and find emotionally healthy spirituality. Through Christ we pray. Amen

52

Commitment Sunday

NOVEMBER 16, 2012

This coming Sunday our congregation will observe COMMITMENT SUNDAY. Commitment Sunday is an opportunity for us as Christians to give thanks to God for his love and provisions which have brought us to this point in our journey. Out of gratitude for what God has done, and all that God has given to us, we now make a commitment of our lives and resources unto God as we look into an upcoming new calendar year. Part of that is a commitment of a portion of our financial resources unto the work of God through Christ's church. We are blessed to be a blessing. We are grateful for the opportunity to be invited by God to share in His ministry. We give, then, because lives are being changed. We give because it is an opportunity and a joy to do so. And, we give because we, being created in the image of God, have an innate need to give.

Some years back, while serving another congregation as pastor, I had a member who taught me a lot about generous, joyful giving. George would often approach me, place some cash in my hand, and say, "Preacher, give this to somebody who needs it more than I do." After doing this several times, I asked George one day, "George, you are such a giving and generous person. Where did you learn this generosity?" Without hesitation he replied, "My Granddad. My Granddad often told me, 'George, you can never out give God.' And, preacher, I have found this to be so true. I have always been blessed by giving."

We are blessed when we give. Jesus said it like this, "It is more blessed to give than to receive." It is a privilege to give. There is actually a God-placed need within us to give. What a privilege to be a part of giving in Jesus' name!

The human heart is a wonderful, amazing organ! It pumps blood in at one valve and then sends it out through another valve. It never stores up blood. It is constantly circulating throughout the body. It gets blood; then it gives blood. It never stores it up for use at a later date. It receives then it gives. The very same is true of any healthy person or healthy church. First, we receive from God....then, with gratitude we graciously give.

Scripture: 2 Corinthians 8:1-5.

Reflection: "They exceeded our expectations, because they gave themselves to the Lord first and to us, consistent with God's will." (2 Corinthians 8:5).

Prayer: O God, because you gave yourself to us, supremely through your Holy Son, we are able in response to reach out and give. Because you love us, we are enabled to love. Creator Lord, everything we have and are is from you. We own nothing, not even our lives. As you have loaned life and gifts to us, may we O Lord, employ all to your honor and glory with joy in our hearts. Amen

53

Happy New Year!

JANUARY 4, 2013

Perhaps we would consider making some promises rather than resolutions for this New Year? Following is a suggested list to prime our pump on promises:

Promise to help your friends believe that there is something special about them.

Promise to attempt to look on the sunny side of life.

Promise to think only of the best, to work only for the best, and to help make the best come true.

Promise to be just as enthusiastic about the success of others as you are about your own.

Promise to forget the mistakes of the past and press on to greater things in the future.

Promise to give so much effort to the improvement of yourself that you have no time to criticize others.

Promise to be too big for worry, too noble for revenge, too joy-filled to permit the presence of negativity in your life.

Should we truly practice these promises it is very likely that we will indeed experience a happy New Year!

Scripture: I Thessalonians 5:14-23.

Reflection: As you take inventory of your life where do you see progress? Celebrate baby steps!

Prayer: God, thank you for fresh starts and new beginnings! In and through you new beginnings are possible every day.

54

Interruption or Inspiration?

FEBRUARY 8, 2013

Today I stopped at the hometown restaurant that I often frequent for lunch. I had just taken the first bite of a sandwich and was looking forward to some quiet time of reading the local paper, when I heard the voice. She was speaking to me. So as not to be rude I looked up and smiled and said "hi" to the young lady who was wiping tables near where I sat. "How are you today?" "Is your meal good, so far?" I thought to myself, can't you see I've just taken the first bite and I am reading the newspaper. But that obviously did not stop her barrage of questions: "Are you having a good day?" "Are you preparing for Sunday's sermon?" (I mentioned that I frequent this eating establishment often!). I nodded in response and attempted to go on with my meal and reading. But today for some reason she would not let up on the questions and conversation.

After asking several more questions she finally moved to another section to clean more tables. I sighed in relief. Then, about five minutes later she came back over to my table. I saw her coming out of the corner of my eye. As she approached my table she said, "Pastor, Sue (one of her co-workers) would like a Bible. She doesn't have one. Could you get her a Bible?" Swallowing my sandwich and my self-centeredness I replied, "Of course. Yes, I'll see that Sue gets a Bible. Thank you for asking!"

I have prayed many times that God would speak through me, use me, in whatever ways to help spread the good news of Jesus right in our own community. And what I perceived as an interruption to my meal and my reading today by a young lady cleaning tables became an avenue of inspiration and a venue of touching someone's life perhaps abundantly and eternally!

Scripture: Matthew 19:13-15.

Reflection: Interruptions may be sources of inspiration.

Prayer: Lord, in the organizing and planning of our days, help us to recognize and affirm that you are the ultimate Planner. You have things to show us and lessons to teach us that cannot be confined, nor limited, to our self-made calendars and self-centered schedules. Open our eyes to see that what we deem an interruption of our day could indeed be an opportunity for service and inspiration. May it be so. Amen

55

Self-Inventory Time

MARCH 29, 2013

I am writing this blog on Good Friday at about 3:45pm. According to the biblical account, Jesus was taken off the cross about 45 minutes ago on that awful day in history! Not only did Jesus suffer the physical agony of the cross, he also had to deal with the rude relationship reality that included his Twelve (with the exception of John) deserting him at his most vulnerable and humiliating experience on this earth!

Over the final couple of days of Jesus' earthly life his closest and dearest followers deserted him, denied him, betrayed him and sold him for thirty pieces of silver! Then, they end up sequestered behind barricaded locked doors in a prison of fear.

While it would be easy to point fingers and aim disparaging words at these original disciples, I believe it would behoove us to use this occasion to do some serious self-inventory. How do you and I betray Jesus? How do we desert and deny Christ? Where in our life and value system have we sold out to something, or someone, in essence creating an idol or addiction in our own world? To be painfully honest, where and when have we crucified Jesus Christ?

In the words of a song, "Does he still feel the nails every time I fail? Does he hear the crowd cry 'crucify" again? Am I causing him pain then I know I've got to change....."

O God, help us to be changed by the Christ of the cross!

Scripture: Matthew 26:14-16.

Reflection: Exam time – In what ways has my life pained God? Confession time – Give this brokenness to God. Grace time – Experience and receive God's healing forgiveness and grace.

Prayer: I wish, Lord, that I could say that as one of your children I have never pained you nor let you down. But, what an exaggerated, unreal wish! I am one of your slow-learning dependents, Father, forgive. Instead, what I really need to say is, Father, forgive me for I have sinned. In that is reality. In that comes reconciliation. In that arrives grace. Thank you, Lord! Amen

56

Termite Teachings

APRIL 26, 2013

Two weeks back I walked into the basement of our mountain cabin ready to do some serious, and much-needed, cleaning out of some junk and clutter. As I picked up some boards that were stacked in a back corner, immediately they began to crumble into pieces onto the basement floor. Something had invaded our home and had begun to work their damage. I didn't know exactly what the intruders were but I had an idea. And, that idea prompted me to call "pest patrol." My idea and concerns were confirmed by the professional - we did, indeed, have termites! A plan is now in place to do some radical and invasive treatment of the home so that these parasitic pests will be eradicated.

Someone has cleverly stated that when it comes to church conflict and disunity "more damage is done by termites on the inside than by woodpeckers on the outside." The termites quietly and stealthily go about their slow, but certain, damage and destruction. The woodpeckers are loud and obvious and therefore easily identified and confronted.

The termite damage mode reminds and teaches us that there are seemingly silent and underground habits, behaviors, and attitudes that can so easily move into our life and begin to set up residence there. At first, we do not even notice the presence of "demons" like anger, bitterness, jealousy, lust taking root....yet, they have moved in and they begin their insidious damage, which can, if not treated, lead to great destruction. There is required of us a vigilant awareness and a healthy dependency upon our Creator and Savior in order to find freedom, healthy spirituality, and forward momentum in our Christ-following walk. One of the best and proven methods of "demon pest" prevention is the regular and frequent practice of spiritual disciplines - i.e. Bible reading and reflection; prayer; holy communion; holy conferencing; fasting; worship; meditation, etc.

These disciplines, through God's power and grace, have the great potential of uncovering and confronting unconscious places in our heart, mind and soul; and providing us with the radical and invasive treatment that is sometimes required.

May termite teachings lead us to a lesson of vigilance and integrity as we continue our faith journey.

Scripture: I Thessalonians 5:5-6; I Peter 5:8.

Reflection: As we think about our respective church family consider: More damage is done by termites on the inside than by woodpeckers on the outside.

Prayer: God, forgive us when we in your family become our own worst enemies! Keep us from biting and devouring one another in the Body of Christ. May we always remember that our unity in Christ, especially in the midst of conflict (which will inevitably occur), is the greatest and most positive witness to the efficacy and joy of the Kingdom. In Jesus, the Prince of Peace, we pray. Amen

57

Elijah Experiences!

JUNE 7, 2013

Currently, during worship time, our congregation is looking at and reflecting upon the life of the prophet Elijah. The Elijah stories are another example to me of the down-to-earth, tell-it-like-it-is messages and narratives in the Bible. The Bible is so real! Our life story is truly in the scriptures! And, Elijah experiences further bear out this truth.

For example, in the 17th chapter of I Kings, Elijah is on the run from King Ahab after sharing some not-so-good news with the King. Elijah is in the wilderness living off provisions providentially provided through the ravens and drinking from a brook. But, with a drought the brook dries up and God sends Elijah to of all places the pagan-dominated town of Zarephath. There the exhausted, refugee, parched Elijah is rescued, as God's word directs, through a poor, disenfranchised widow!

Elijah's experience reminds us that we never know what our next day, our next experience, may hold. One day, along with Elijah, life finds us doing great, in the King's court - a place of power and influence and comfort. And, next, life takes us to the wilderness. Next, we make our way out of the wilderness only to land in a strange place with strangers all around us. Yet, in the midst of all these changes and difficulties, God continues to be present and God has a word for us....and, perhaps a word we might share with others. In the most unusual way; in unexplainable and uncontainable methods God is present and speaking a word which provides and delivers; renews and rescues.

Later, in the Elijah experiences, in I Kings chapter 19, Elijah has just participated in the astounding Yahweh victory over the Baal prophets on Mount Carmel. What a powerful and awesome display of God's power and might! And as Elijah comes down off of Carmel he learns that Queen Jezebel is coming after him. So, he flees, once again, to the wilderness in fear! In the wilderness and barrenness of desert and of spirit Elijah becomes depressed and even suicidal. He is spiritually, emotionally, and physically exhausted and depleted. But the angel of the Lord comes to Elijah and brings help and hope. It strikes me that the first advice that the angel of the Lord gives to broken, exhausted Elijah is NOT a prayer lesson. Nor does the angel give a lecture on spiritual perseverance. Instead, the angel instructs Elijah to eat and rest; and, then, a second time to eat and to rest.

The struggles of life, the rhythm of life, which we ignore at our own peril; and, the wholeness of life to which God created us for, and called us to, are evidenced in the Elijah experiences. God meets us in all our experiences - be they mountain top or wilderness -seeking to shape us and use us for Kingdom work. Sometimes that Kingdom work involves spiritual victory on a mountain top; sometimes it is reflection and waiting in the wilderness; and, sometimes it is the self-care and provision of God through sabbath rest and nourishment for our bodies.

Scripture: I Kings 19

Reflection: "Even though I walk through the darkest of valleys, I will fear no evil, for you, O Lord, are with me." Psalm 23:4

Prayer: Life throws us curves, Lord. Only you are the same yesterday, today, and forever. May our trust always be in you. Amen

58

On Witnessing

JULY 15, 2013

It seems like we Christians often make witnessing for Jesus complicated and unnatural when authentic witnessing is simple (although not easy or without effort) and natural. Recently, reading and reflecting upon Luke's gospel, chapter 10, where Jesus sends out the seventy-two, two-by-two, I discovered these helpful witnessing take-aways -

- Go out in God's AUTHORITY (vs. 1, 19)
- Go out with SIMPLICTY (vs 4)
  - Travel Light
  - Leave "Baggage" behind
- Go out remembering your first PRIORITY (v. 4b)
  - Stay focused
- Go out RELATIONALLY (vss. 5-11)
  - Mingle with culture; avoid isolationism
- Go out in UNITY (v. 1)
  - We are not alone in this mission. Gather to scatter!
- Come back in genuine HUMILITY (vss. 17-20)
  - Practice "Bold Humility" in Jesus' name!

Let your light shine!

Scripture: Luke 10:1-24

Reflection: We are gathered in order to be scattered.

Prayer: O Lord our God, Light of the world, as your community of faith, may we go deeper into your holy Word, that we may, as a result, go wider into your needy world, sharing the life and the light of Jesus the Christ, in whom we pray. Amen

59

On Becoming a Grandparent!

AUGUST 5, 2013

Through the years I have heard newly become grandparents pronounce things like: "Wow! Being a grandparent is one of the greatest things in the world!" "You get to spoil your grandchildren and then send them home!" "If I had known that grandparenting was this much fun I would have had my grandchildren before I had my children!"

I would hear these statements and try to smile along with the one speaking, thinking possibly they're making the obligatory and perfunctory grandparent statements. But then....then...Wesley David Kurtz was born. Our first grandchild had arrived! He even had the courtesy and kindness of being born on a Sunday evening while we were on vacation! Had it been another Sunday (as Karen and I are both pastors of a local church and Sundays obviously keep us occupied) Karen and I would not have been able to be in attendance in the waiting area during the birthing at a Raleigh, NC hospital! Way to go Wesley!

On Sunday evening, July 21st Wesley came into this world! His Dad and Mom were troopers and the result was an 8 pound, 9 ounce beautiful boy! Less than an hour after he was born I got to lay my eyes on him and say a blessing over him!

Now I'm a believer! I understand and experience all those "grandparent" statements and sentiments....because I have fallen in love again! Thank you God! And, thank you Wesley!

Scripture: Luke 2:36-38.

Reflection: Thanks be to God for grandchildren and grandparents!

Prayer: Lord, may your Word and your grace be extended from generation to generation. Amen

60

Finding Sabbath Time Under the Stars
SEPTEMBER 27, 2013

Lately things have seemingly gotten extra busy in my life - - a lot of changes and with it many tasks and responsibilities. Have you noticed, the busier we get, often times, the less time we take for sabbath and renewal time. Ironically, at our busiest seasons is when we require sabbath the most yet observe Sabbath the least!

Wayne Muller, in his book appropriately titled "Sabbath," shares, "Sabbath time is a revolutionary challenge to the violence of overwork, because it honors the necessary wisdom of dormancy. During Sabbath is when we have the opportunity and deep need to take our hand from the plow and let the earth care for things, while we drink, if just briefly, from the fountain of rest and delight."

Over the past several months, Karen and I have discovered a wonderful sabbath time. Many weeks this past summer, and now into the autumn season, we take a couple lawn chairs, a citronella candle, and our tired beings....and we sit (often in silence) and we simply watch night fall. It seems so simple. Why did I not think of this before?!

We are hearing and seeing things in God's creation that we did not see and hear before! The birds; the deer; the cicadas; the cloud patterns overhead; the distinctiveness of each tree around us! Oh, yes, and the presence of one another! Sometimes the connection comes from being together in silence. At other times we process the day. Being, instead of doing! Resting, not working! Stillness, not moving! Reflecting, not producing! And as darkness settles in we are finding sabbath time under the stars!

Scripture: Exodus 20:8; Exodus 34:21; Luke 2:23-28.

Reflection: To sit still is to practice Sabbath, which means, literally to stop.

Prayer: Days pass and the years vanish and we walk sightless among miracles. Lord, fill our eyes with seeing and our minds with knowing. Let there be moments when your Presence, like lightning, illumines the darkness in which we walk. Help us to see, wherever we gaze, that the bush burns, unconsumed. And we, clay touched by God, will reach out for holiness and exclaim in wonder, "How filled with awe is this place and we did not know it." -Mishkan Tefilah, From the Jewish Sabbath Prayer Book

61

A New Ministry Space Opens!

NOVEMBER 8, 2013

God has blessed our congregation with a brand new multi-purpose ministry space! It just opened this week. After being on the envisioning master plan drawings for more than ten years; after being in the planning stages for over five years, thanks be to God, it is now reality! The words of King Solomon ring in my ears as he was before the people of God dedicating the Lord's new Temple in Israel! Solomon prayed and petitioned God's blessing upon those who entered that sacred space AND he also prayed that through this space the foreigner and the stranger might also find an acceptance and a blessing!

This new ministry space has required a lot of prayers, dreams, plans, discussions, energy, time and meetings. But somehow, some way it has happened. And now, in reality, the important work is just beginning. Namely, to fill the space with ministries and missions that will change lives and make followers of Jesus Christ! We have said all along that this building is NOT the end game. It is only a ministry tool. It is a means to an end - making disciples of Jesus Christ.

Like Solomon; like the dedication of the Temple in Jerusalem, may God's blessing be showered upon those who enter this ministry space and may those we do not even know (the stranger and the guest) and those who, as of yet, are not even born, find here an acceptance and a blessing.

Scripture: I Chronicles 5 and 6.

Reflection: The church is not a building. The church is the people of Jesus Christ. A brick and mortar building is only a tool for ministry and mission.

Prayer: Thank you, Lord, for the resources you entrust to us for use in your Kingdom! May we always realize that the church is not a building; rather, the church is your people gathered and scattered in your name. What a blessing it is to have a designated and dedicated space in which to gather, worship and fellowship in Jesus' name. Yet, these building resources and tools are never intended as fortresses in which to hide or cloisters in which to cocoon from the world. Instead, they are places in which we receive nourishment and nurture as Christ sends us out and onward on our journeys in this world. Amen

62

The Light of Bethlehem Shines in the Darkness

DECEMBER 7, 2013

This Advent-Christmas Season I have been spending time reflecting upon a particular phrase that has captured my attention: The Light of Bethlehem shines in the darkness. I have been preparing a series of Advent messages dwelling upon this same theme. Into the darkness of our despair shines the Bethlehem light of hope. Into the darkness of our deepest anxieties shines the Bethlehem light of peace. Into the darkness of our fear shines the Bethlehem light of joy. And, into the darkness of our hate shines the Bethlehem light of love. The Light of Bethlehem, the Light of the world, Jesus the Christ, shines into our darkness and brings hope, peace, joy and love. Traditionally, these are the titles of the four candles on our Advent wreaths, reminding us of the hope, peace, joy and love which guides us - A hope, peace, joy and love to sustain in the very center of darkness; a hope, peace, joy and love to share.

Growing up, one of my favorite Appalachian carols (which remains one of my favorite Christmas songs) was "Beautiful Star of Bethlehem." Be blessed as you reflect upon these hope-filled lyrics:

Oh, beautiful Star of Bethlehem, shining afar thru shadows dim, giving a light for those who long have gone. And guiding the wise men on their way unto the place where Jesus lay, Beautiful Star of Bethlehem shine on.

Chorus: Oh, beautiful Star of Bethlehem, shine upon us until the glory dawn. Oh, give us thy light to light the way unto the land of perfect day, beautiful Star of Bethlehem, shine on.

Oh, beautiful Star, the hope of light, guiding the pilgrim through the night, over the mountain till the break of dawn, and into the light of perfect day, it will give out a lovely ray, beautiful Star of Bethlehem shine on.

Oh, beautiful Star, the hope of rest, for the redeemed the good and blest, yonder in glory when the crown is won; for Jesus is now that Star divine, brighter and brighter he will shine, beautiful Star of Bethlehem shine on.

May the Star, the Light, of Bethlehem shine hope, peace, joy and love upon you this Advent-Christmas Season and always.

Scripture: Matthew 2:1-2; John 1:1-5.

Reflection: In the Bible, the Star of Bethlehem, also traditionally called the Christmas Star, revealed the birth of Jesus to the Magi.

Prayer: Light of the World, into our despair, shine hope. Into our deepest anxieties, shine peace. Into our fear, shine joy. And into our hate, shine love. In the name of the Father, the Son, and the Holy Spirit. Amen

63

Baptism of Grandson!

JANUARY 3, 2014

This past Sunday, Karen and I had one of the great privileges of a lifetime - - we baptized our grandson, Wesley David Kurtz! I wanted to freeze the moments (kairos moments as opposed to chronos time). Asking the faith commitment questions of Wesley's parents - Joshua and Tara; pouring the water into the baptismal font; holding Wesley in my arms and placing water upon his head - the mark of our identity and belonging in Christ; praying a prayer over Wesley and his life in Jesus; carrying Wesley out into the congregation; participating as a congregation in the remembering or anticipating of our own baptism. And, then the congregation shared together the Apostles' Creed. Wow! It was so overwhelming and so inspiring! The community of faith - what a privilege, through God's grace, to belong, to be a part of the family of God! As we baptized Wesley I was reminded again of this precious gift of being invited into the family of God. Baptism, the sacrament (sacred gift) of initiation into the community of faith is offered to us all. Wesley, and each of us, is not alone in this Christian pilgrimage. Immanuel, God is with us. And we have one another to support, encourage and guide in this journey. Baptism is the great "Amen!" to God's gracious invitation and initiation of love. In baptism we say "Yes!" to the Holy Trinity's awesome invite into the family of faith!

Wesley, you are loved with an everlasting love! You are a part of a family, a community, of faith that is blessed beyond measure – a community that is blessed to be a blessing!

Scripture: Luke 2:25-35.

Reflection: In the waters of holy baptism God names us, claims us, and ordains us to ministry as his people.

Prayer: Now, master, let your servant depart in peace according to your word, because my eyes have seen your salvation. – The prayer of Simeon in the Temple while holding the baby Jesus in his arms.

64

Life-Giving Water!

JANUARY 31, 2014

I recently returned from a pilgrimage to the Holy Land. It was interesting to me, and ironic, that the Land in which water is relatively scarce became that which we focused upon, and spent a great deal of our time in and on - - the water!

A large part of our first day, of 10 days, was spent on a boat out on the Sea of Galilee. At one point we anchored out on the Lake and worshipped and shared together the sacrament of Holy Communion. What an incredible experience, looking to the backdrop of the shoreline of that Sea where Jesus had called his very first followers while we broke bread and drank from the cup!

Later on our journey, we travelled to the Jordan River. There, many of us donned white robes and were immersed in the waters of that same River where John the Baptist baptized Jesus. As we came up out of the water we heard the words, "Remember you baptism and be thankful!"

Toward the end of our pilgrimage we made our way to the Dead Sea. Here we floated on our backs in the waters so thick with salt and minerals that the buoyancy of the water kept one afloat without effort. The Dead Sea is so named because it cannot sustain life. Water flows in, but no water exits. Therefore it is appropriately named "Dead." This is analogous to a life that receives but doesn't give.

Jesus, who walked this same Israel geography in the first century, was acutely aware of the preciousness and rarity of water, and yet essentialness of this same water to life and living. This same Jesus, meeting a Samaritan woman at a well, spoke to her and to us of Living Water as he shares, "People soon become thirsty again after drinking this (physical) water. But the water (eternal and living) I give them takes away thirst altogether. It becomes a perpetual spring within them, giving them eternal life."

Let us drink deeply and continually of the Living Water!

Scripture: John 4:4-14; John 7:37-38.

Reflection: What H2O can do for our bodies, Jesus can do for our hearts!

Prayer: Lord, I come thirsty. I come to drink, to receive. I receive your work on the cross and in your resurrection. My sins are pardoned, and my death is defeated. I receive your energy. Empowered by your Holy Spirit, I can do all things through Christ, who gives me strength. I receive your lordship. I belong to you. Nothing comes to me that has not passed through you. And I receive your love. Nothing can separate me from your love. –Max Lucado

65

Decisions in the Desert

MARCH 7, 2014

We have just recently entered into the season of Lent as communicated on the Christian calendar. Lent is often perceived as a time to give up something, a negative season, almost a pejorative term. Yet, I suggest nothing could be further from the truth! Lent is a gift from heaven; a blessing from God. While the Lenten Season may be compared to a "wilderness time" or a "desert time," agreed, desert time offers and calls for a time of intentional reflection and examination before God. There are at least two wonderful qualities that are offered in the wilderness and desert times. They are the simple and basic spiritual disciplines (yet, not easy and counter cultural) of observing solitude and silence. Solitude and silence - that which we need consistently are the very same from which we flee frequently! Our lives are overloaded and over-stimulated. This, then, is all the more why we need solitude and silence; all the more reason why we need times of reflection and self-examination. As has been stated, "The unexamined life is not worth living." May we receive and embrace this Lenten Season as a holy and sacred gift from God - an opportunity to practice the spiritual disciplines of solitude and silence, contemplation and confession.

Scripture: Psalm 46:10; Mark 6:30-32.

Reflection: Be fed that you may feed others.

Prayer: O God, help us to reframe desert and wilderness times, from something barren, hopeless and useless, into seeing these times as opportunities for re-examination and renewal, out of which new possibilities and creativity are birthed.

66

Looking for Spring!

APRIL 4, 2014

I know that the Bible tells us to, "Be thankful in all things." I try to practice that gratitude spirit with the help and grace of God. I really do. But, I must say that the colder and longer winter weather in our part of the country this year has tried my thanksgiving spirit for the recent weather patterns (Sorry, Lord! I'll try to do better).

We've finally hit some 70-degree plus days! Yes! Bring it on! These are days to bask in the bright, warm sunshine - time to sit out under the evening summer skies. This I have been waiting upon, and hoping for, for a long time. Oh, well, I suppose I would not appreciate this springtime weather near as much if we did not experience a change in seasons - including the cold winds of winter. But, I, for one, am so ready for the warm and gentle breezes of spring!

May this longing for the sunshine and warmth of the spring, remind us of our need of and craving for the warmth and grace of the Son - the Christ! The grace and love of God are there for us, just for the asking and receiving! Sometimes in our coasting through life; in our taking for granted; in the midst of what become idols, addictions, and demons, we drift and we crash. God offers us a better way - much better. God invites us to come out of the cold and dark of sin; and, instead to live in the warmth of his love and the light of his path. I'm reminded of a 1970 song written by Kurt Kaiser. The words go like this:

When in the spring, the flowers are blooming bright and fair, After the grey of winter's gone. Once again the lark begins his tuning, Back in the meadows of my heart.

Chorus: Lord, to my heart bring back the springtime. Take away the cold and dark of sin. And, Oh refill me now, sweet Holy Spirit: May I warm and tender be again.

Lord, make me like that stream that flows so cool and clear, Down from the mountains high above; I will tell the world the wondrous story, Of the precious stream filled with your love.

(Chorus)

May you know, and be blessed by, the warmth of spring!

Scripture: Jeremiah 31:3; I John 3:1.

Reflection: May we bask and rejoice in the love of God!

Prayer: God, our Heavenly Parent, wrap us in your everlasting arms of love! When we would run toward the many loud and alluring voices ringing in our ears, may we come to our senses and run into your arms. Thank you for the security and strength that we find there that empowers us to serve in your world.

67

A Staff Day Apart

JUNE 13, 2014

Recently our staff travelled to a nearby favorite spot - a retreat center - for a day together apart. The word "apart" reminds me of a quotation that is both wise and practical (wisdom, after all, usually is practical and applicable!): "Come apart before you come apart!" Come apart from the routine. Come apart - away - from the usual and the ordinary. Come apart from your labor and your work. Come apart to reflect, to renew, to reconnect with God and with one another. Come apart.

What a difference even seven hours apart can make! During our retreat we shared a couple sessions on how to be a better staff. One of our own staff facilitated this process with the help of a video format. We discussed and reflected upon how we might be better servants to one another as servant leaders. The idea was not to level the positional flow chart; but, rather, no matter our position or title, to be of service to one another as Christ followers. This seemed to be a fruitful discussion with a couple applicable "take-aways" for our staff team.

We also took some time for informal fellowship - eating a leisurely noon meal; taking some walks through the nearby wooded trails; and some time for being alone with God.

Some might say, "What a wasted time. Think of all you could have gotten done that you did not do, as concerns the various job descriptions!" However, I could not disagree more, because the renewed perspective and renewed relationships gleaned through this day retreat granted through this time apart provide inspiration and encouragement to staff members that will serve a positive purpose for a long time. Remember to take time to "come apart before you come apart."

Scripture: Matthew 14:22-23.

Reflection: Rest, reflection, and retreat can lend proper perspective and renewal of one's call.

Prayer: Jesus, you, who were God on earth, often carved out time to be alone with your Heavenly Father and with your followers. If you needed this retreat time from the pressures and the cares and the loud voices of the world, how much more do we need this time apart! Help us to do that for which our souls crave – spending time with you, O Lord.

68

Time with Mom

JULY 11, 2014

About every three weeks or so I make a drive up to the Blue Ridge Mountains and check in with my Mom. Our family is greatly blessed to continue having Mom with us! Mom turned 89 years of age last week and she possesses amazing energy and agility for her age! I was with her yesterday and we played our usual game of Skip-Bo and then I took her out to one of her favorite restaurants for a luncheon together. In the course of our lunch conversation she confided how she was slowing down. In almost the very same breath she told me that this particular week she had delivered meals on wheels three days (a thirty-six mile trek to 15 to 20 homes delivering hot meals); worked out at an exercise center two days; swept out her garage and sidewalk and pulled some weeds in her flower garden; did a load of laundry; got in the neighbor's mail while they were on vacation; and, took her "aged" friend out to eat! Well, I suppose "slowing down" is a relative term....at least it seems so with my relatives!

Yet, truthfully, in some ways Mom has slowed down. But, you know, I love it. Because it allows some quality time to be spent together to better get to know and appreciate my Mom. Don't get me wrong I have always loved and appreciated her (well, my teen years I may have been like a lot of teens "psychotic" - so probably not appreciating Mom then like I should have); but now with her slowing down a bit, she sits and talks for longer periods of time than ever I remember during my growing up days. And, she now talks on the phone for a long time! In fact, I can hardly get off the phone with Mom these days - which is a wonderful thing.

Mom, I am forever grateful to God for you! I treasure the occasions we are privileged to spend, no invest, time together - the every three weeks, or so, of playing Skip-Bo, Rummikub; visiting; going out to eat meals; and simply talking and sharing life. I'm so glad you have finally slowed down!

Scripture: Exodus 20:12.

Reflection: In what ways are we honoring our parents – whether they are living or deceased?

Prayer: Lord, may we respect and honor our parents. They have their limitations and faults, like we all do. But they are the parents you have given us. May they be blessed through our words and by our actions. Amen

69

When Empty Is A Good Thing

AUGUST 8, 2014

Our contemporary life seems so "filled with filling"! We fill silence with noise and words. We fill schedules with activities. We fill paper with print. We fill days with events. We often attempt to fill our time with all the novel, exciting, self-fulfilling experiences we could possibly cram into one 24-hour period so that we do not miss out on life and all that life has to offer!

It is not necessarily that these "fillings" are bad, in and of themselves. But the liability enters when we continue day after day and season after season to fill and fill and fill, with no, or very little, time to intentionally and purposefully empty. By purposefully empty I mean emptying of ourselves; detoxing from our rush; silencing the inner noise so that we may re-calibrate and re-focus by the leading of our Creator. This is emptying with the intent and purpose of being filled with the things that really matter. I submit that there is a world of difference between just emptying and emptying with the motive and desire to be filled with the things of God. Perhaps our prayer would simply be, "Come, Lord Jesus, fill my life with the things that truly matter so that I may be filled to overflowing with your grace and peace," or something similar.

Recently I took vacation with my family. Not all vacations have been renewing for me, for a variety of reasons. But this one was. I was able to find some much-needed emptying on this get away. When I reflect upon why this was true, some of the reason, I affirm, was that this vacation was simple. We had very few plans during the entire week. Each person could do pretty much their own thing. If together, fine. If alone, fine too. The setting was simple and beautiful. It was in the mountains - a lot of time spent hiking on trails and leisurely kayaking on a lake - in God's natural creation. Imagine! Natural....Simple....Low key! It was one of the best times ever! And through the emptying I was filled up, in order to be re-loaded and re-newed and re-conciled!

Today I looked up the word "vacate," from which comes our word vacation. My dictionary reveals: Vacate - To leave vacant or cease to occupy. Reflect again with me on the meaning of vacate - To leave; to cease; to empty. Part of the written staff covenant for our church staff says, "Divert daily; withdraw weekly; and, abandon annually." In this covenant we remind ourselves as staff members that we need to make and take time, in our over-filled world, to empty - empty of ourselves and of our stuff - so that we may have room to be filled with the things that truly matter.

Scripture: Philippians 1:11; Colossians 1:9; Ephesians 3:19.

Reflection: Divert daily; withdraw weekly; and, abandon annually.

Prayer: Come, Lord Jesus, fill my life with the things that truly matter so that I may be filled to overflowing with your grace and peace. Amen

70

Easter People!

Recently during a worship service at Oak Ridge UMC we were all invited and encouraged to look for "God-sightings" in our daily life and living - - places, relationships, and experiences where we see God through the eyes of faith; places where we see evidence of God and of God's working. It is amazing what we find when we look for it! By being intentional about this "faith task" of looking for God-sightings, I found myself perceiving God in new yet "ordinary" ways. It is a task and perspective that should be practiced every day! In the words of Jesus, "Blessed are your eyes, because they see.." (Matthew 13:16)

Jesus, our resurrected Lord, is alive and at work in our world! May we have our eyes of faith opened....and see!

What a powerful moment that very first Easter morning when Mary Magdelene encountered the living, resurrected Lord Jesus Christ! Mary had come to the tomb of Jesus grieving over his loss and his death. Read again the powerful scene at the cemetery:

Jesus: Why are you crying? Who are you looking for?

Mary: Sir (thinking he was the gardener), if you have taken him away, tell me where you have put him, and I will go and get him.

Jesus: Mary!

Mary: Teacher!

What a powerful encounter with the resurrected Savior! Mary thought Jesus was dead and gone, but he is alive and there before her very eyes! What an unforgettable, and life-changing, God-sighting!

How can we describe and explain something so incredible and so wonderful and awesome?! Human words cannot do justice.

Joe LoMusio, in his book "If I Should Die Before I Live" relates:

If I were to ask you to describe Easter without using any words, you could only use punctuation marks, which punctuation mark would you chose to describe this Easter for yourself? Maybe this Easter is a comma for you. It makes you stop, pause, think, and listen, but that's about it. Perhaps today is a downer - a big bold period. You thought you'd feel excited, but instead it seems to be more like empty ritual. You feel like you're not on the inside, but on the outside...an onlooker.

It was a day when life felt like a period for Jesus' disciples. He was dead. He was buried. An end to expectations. But wait - news of an empty tomb...the period is no longer a period, it's a question mark. That's worse than a period. Now they're beginning to doubt. Where is He? They're perplexed. The guards are gone, the stone is rolled away. He is not there. And if not there, where?

An angel speaks, "Why do you seek the living One among the dead? He is not here, but He has risen. Remember how He spoke to you while He was in Galilee, saying that the Son of Man must be delivered into the hands of sinful men, and how He must be crucified, and the third day He must rise again." Of course they remembered! The periods are gone. The question marks are removed. There is one massive exclamation point!

That's what Easter in all about...an exclamation of gratitude and of praise for the resurrection of Jesus Christ and for the salvation His victory over death brought to us.

Scripture: John 20.

Reflection: The resurrection of Jesus Christ confirms our hope and assures our victory!

Prayer: Resurrected Lord, through the power of God the grave could not contain you. Death could not defeat you. And now the condition and promise is offered: those who die to self in Christ shall be raised to life in Christ! They shall become Easter people.